Better

UNDER PRESSURE

Better
UNDER PRESSURE

How Great Leaders

Bring Out the Best

in Themselves and Others

Justin Menkes

HARVARD BUSINESS REVIEW PRESS

Boston, Massachusetts

Library of Congress Cataloging-in-Publication Data
Menkes, Justin.
  Better under pressure : how great leaders bring out the best in themselves
and others / Justin Menkes.
    p. cm.
  ISBN 978-1-4221-3870-0 (hardcover : alk. paper)   1. Executive ability.
2. Leadership.   I. Title.
  HD38.2.M46227 2011
  658.4'092—dc22   2010047556

The paper used in this publication meets the requirements of the American
National Standard for Permanence of Paper for Publications and Documents
in Libraries and Archives Z39.48-1992.

For Susan, my favorite.

Contents

Acknowledgments

My colleagues at Spencer Stuart: the most talented collection of people I've ever known.

Tom Neff and David Daniel: their support of this project made it possible.

Nick Young: a brother to me.

Ania Wieckowski, Jacque Murphy, and the rest of Harvard's staff: they took this material to another level.

Lucy McCauley: she is a master of her editorial craft.

Rafe Sagalyn: one of my most trusted advisors.

The people quoted in this book were only a fraction of those that helped form the ideas. I cannot express enough gratitude to all that were so gracious with their time and patient with my questions. I must express a special thanks to the following:

Richard H. Anderson	Chief Executive Officer	Delta Airlines
Clive J. Beddoe	Executive Chairman	WestJet Airlines
Gordon Bethune	Former Chief Executive Officer	Continental Airlines
Lawrence J. Blanford	Chief Executive Officer	Green Mountain Coffee Roasters
Thomas Andrew Boardman	Chief Executive Officer	Nedbank Ltd.

Lawrence A. Bossidy	Former Chairman and Chief Executive Officer	Honeywell International, Inc.
Gregory C. Case	Chief Executive Officer	Aon Corporation
Patrick C. Daniel	President and Chief Executive Officer	Enbridge, Inc.
Ronald D. Daniel	Former Managing Director	McKinsey & Company, Inc.
Dr. Marijn M. Dekkers	Chief Executive Officer	Bayer AG
Michael Dell	Chairman and Chief Executive Officer	Dell Computers
David C. Denison	Chief Executive Officer	Canada Pension Plan Investment Board
David B. Dillon	Chairman and Chief Executive Officer	Kroger Company
John A. Edwardson	Chairman and Chief Executive Officer	CDW Corporation
Darren Entwistle	President and Chief Executive Officer	Tellus Corporation
Mark P. Frissora	Chairman and Chief Executive Officer	Hertz Corporation
James L. Hambrick	Chairman, President and Chief Executive Officer	Lubrizol Corporation
Fred Hassan	Chairman and Chief Executive Officer	Schering-Plough Corporation
Andrea Jung	Chairman and Chief Executive Officer	Avon, Inc.
Christopher J. Kearney	Chairman, President and Chief Executive Officer	SPX Corporation
Herbert D. Kelleher	Former Chairman and Chief Executive Officer	Southwest Airlines
Richard L. Keyser	Former Chief Executive Officer	W.W. Grainger, Inc.
James M. Kilts	Former Chairman, President and Chief Executive Officer	Gillette Company
Jeffrey B. Kindler, Jr. Esq.	Chairman and Chief Executive Officer	Pfizer

Alan G. Lafley	Former Chairman and Chief Executive Officer	Procter & Gamble Company
Jacques Lamarre	President and Chief Executive Officer	SNC-Lavalin Group, Inc.
Ralph Larsen	Chairman and Chief Executive Officer	Johnson & Johnson
Richard H. Lenny	Former Chairman, President and Chief Executive Officer	Hershey Company
James McNulty	Chairman and Former Chief Executive Officer	Parsons Corporation
Raymond J. Milchovich	Chairman and Chief Executive Officer	Foster Wheeler, Ltd.
James F. Mooney	Chairman	Virgin Media, Inc.
David C. Novak	Chairman and Chief Executive Officer	Yum! Brands, Inc.
Neil S. Novich	Chairman, President and Chief Executive Officer	Ryerson Steel
David J. O'Reilly	Former President and Chief Executive Officer	Chevron Corporation
James W. Owens	Former Chairman and Chief Executive Officer	Caterpillar Inc.
Gregory R. Page	Chairman, President and Chief Executive Officer	Cargill, Inc.
William D. Perez	Former Chairman and Chief Executive Officer	William Wrigley Jr. Company
Steven S. Reinemund	Former Chairman and Chief Executive Officer	PepsiCo, Inc.
Irene B. Rosenfeld	Chairman and Chief Executive Officer	Kraft Inc.
Thomas M. Ryan	Chairman, President and Chief Executive Officer	CVS/Caremark Corporation
Paolo Scaroni	Managing Director and Chief Executive Officer	ENI S.p.A.
Henry B. Schacht	Partner and Senior Advisor	Warburg Pincus LLC
Ivan G. Seidenberg	Chairman and Chief Executive Officer	Verizon Communications Corporation

Kevin W. Sharer	Chairman and Chief Executive Officer	Amgen, Inc.
Jim Skinner	Vice Chairman and Chief Executive Officer	McDonald's Corporation
Frederick W. Smith	Chairman and Chief Executive Officer	FedEx Corporation
David Speer	Chairman and Chief Executive Officer	ITW-Illinois Tool Works
Joseph R. Swedish	President and Chief Executive Officer	Trinity Health Organization
Chris Van Gorder	President and Chief Executive Officer	Scripps Health
William G. Walter	Chairman, President and Chief Executive Officer	FMC Corporation
Richard L. Wambold	Chairman and Chief Executive Officer	Pactiv Corporation
Miles D. White	Chairman and Chief Executive Officer	Abbott Laboratories, Inc.
William D. Zollars	Chairman and Chief Executive Officer	YRC Worldwide Inc.

Better
UNDER PRESSURE

Introduction

Great Leadership in a World of Ongoing Duress

As I sat in the conference room of one of the largest companies in the world, the board members and the CEO and chairman were nodding their heads in agreement to several statements written on a white board in front of us. We had spent the last two days going through a process my colleagues and I facilitate at the beginning of every CEO succession effort—identifying all of the strategic challenges facing the business, and thus the skills the CEO's successor would most need to thrive. The list of challenges, any of which would mean a massive, fundamental shift in the company's ability to make money, included items such as these:

- Nationalistic movements in countries where our production is based threaten to renegotiate our contracts or annex our facilities outright, threatening 70 percent of our supply lines.

- Political leadership is proposing dramatic new taxes on our industry that would radically reduce our profitability.

- Our product is being called a threat to the environment. There-fore, much of our customer base is calling for a sharp reduction of our product's use or its outright replacement within the next decade.

All of the threats on this list of doom were highly plausible. Was this company in trouble? It was. It also happens to be one of the most profitable companies in the history of private enterprise.

The CEO remarked nonchalantly as the group stared at the list, "That looks about right."

That's when the full impact of what I'd been observing at compa-nies over the last decade hit me: no matter how successful, thriving, or seemingly secure any business appears, there are no longer periods of calm seas for leaders in any industry. Leaders today must be at home navigating a ship through forty-foot waves—oceans that will never again be serene—and still be able to guide their crew safely from port to port. In other words, they must continue to be highly ef-fective, particularly in an environment of extraordinary, ongoing stress. They must be better under pressure.

A broader statistic clarifies this point about the new operating envi-ronment: more than half the companies that were industry leaders in 1955 were still industry leaders in 1990. Yet, more than two-thirds of market leaders in 1990 no longer existed by 2004.[1] Bethlehem Steel, Woolworths, Arthur Andersen—all corporate institutions that en-dured for a century or more—have disappeared in the last ten years.

What kind of leader does it take to help companies survive—and thrive—in the midst of such a fundamental shift in the operating en-vironment? What qualities make leaders able to sail through the rolling ocean that is the new normal, and bring their people with them? And how can leaders develop those attributes?

To perform their best in precisely such an atmosphere of multiple ill-defined and ongoing threats to the enterprise's survival, a leader must possess a highly unusual set of attributes that often run counter to natural human behavior. This book, written for leaders and aspiring leaders, will explore those attributes in detail—and show you how you can begin to develop them yourself. These attributes also add up to a new definition of leadership. The definition takes into account the way that all individuals—leaders and the led alike—are influenced by those around them in their quest for success.

A New Definition of Leadership

As a psychologist who works with the world's top CEOs, I have spent the last eight years specifically studying the differences between CEOs who fail and those who have shown remarkable staying power. I've worked with companies as they vet candidates for their top positions, helping them understand the key attributes needed for a person in that position to succeed. The findings in this book are based specifically on in-depth psychological interviews conducted with dozens of CEOs from the world's largest companies, both retired legends and those considered current masters of their domain, as well as analyses of performance evaluations for more than two hundred candidates being considered for chief executive roles.

Two of those conversations in particular help frame the most important lessons about what sets the best leaders apart under today's extreme conditions.

Larry Bossidy, retired chairman and CEO of Honeywell, spoke about the single thing that influenced him most profoundly during his career. "I was always really afraid that I wouldn't succeed," he told me. "I can remember on my mother's deathbed, she said, 'Larry, fulfill your potential.' She did a lot of great things for me over my life, but I've never forgotten what she said. And that's what I was most worried about. Was I going to fulfill my potential? I didn't know what that was—certainly I didn't know I was going to be a CEO for ten years. But I just wanted to make sure that I went as far as I could. And I wanted the same for my people—for them to fulfill their potential."[2]

It is clear that Bossidy, who had led one of the largest companies in the world, was never immune to fear of failure. But when he was in the face of this fear, his mother encouraged him to see the intense gratification that came from rising to ever higher levels of achievement—fulfilling his potential. He remembered this encouragement throughout his career and in turn, he himself became legendary for his ability to teach others how to do the same. Great leaders seek to fulfill their own potential but equally seek to fulfill the potential of those who work for and with them.

Another example comes from the grocery industry. David Dillon's family started a grocery store business in the early 1900s and was highly successful, with four successive generations of Dillons running the company before Dillon eventually became CEO of what we know today as Kroger. Under his leadership, Kroger has maintained a dominant market share in the grocery store business. But the way he got started in the business holds the key to his ongoing success as a leader.

In fact, Dillon had never intended to join the family business. He had planned to practice law, until one day his cousin Dick suggested that he work for the business for a couple of years first. He could gain some valuable experience, the cousin said, that he could apply to anything he decided to do in life if he didn't want to stay. But what finally convinced him was what the cousin said next: "He warned that if I decided to stay after those two years, I'd be on my own and whatever I achieved or didn't achieve would be the result of actual performance—and not because of anything they'd give me. When he said that, that's when I knew I could sign up."[3]

David Dillon thus resolved from an early age to aim for meaningful personal achievement, to pursue a life focused on realizing his potential. Inherited wealth or positions held no interest for him: he was gratified by his own triumph over obstacles, earning achievement through work, and not through connections. And whereas his cousin Dick helped create the *context* for this wisdom to emerge by pointing out to him the conditions for joining the family business, David would later create contexts that helped his people, in turn, experience the gratification and subsequent thirst for self-improvement that comes from overcoming obstacles as a path to meaningful achievement.

This phenomenon has proven itself over decades of modern management. Many years before David Dillon began working to fulfill his own potential and that of those around him, Larry Bossidy had taken to heart his mother's belief in his ability to do the same. Human beings doing their best—and helping others to do their best—are and have always been a key game changer.

In fact, this is the first of the two major points that emerged from my studies: leaders' ability to realize their maximum potential and the potential of their workforce is the most profound way that they can differentiate themselves. It is the essential part of a CEO's job. This represents such a fundamental shift in our perception of leadership that it calls for a new definition. *Leadership* means realizing potential—in yourself and in the people you lead. Yet to be effective, this kind of leadership can't be unidirectional. Rather, leader and followers cocreate their identities and performance. Thus we move away from the old paradigm in which leaders have an impact on their people, who in turn perform. The new paradigm for leadership becomes a fluid, virtuous cycle of exchange and growth between leaders and the people they lead.

The second major point is that because the external environment around leadership has changed dramatically, *how* leaders realize their own and others' potential has changed dramatically as well. Whereas in Bossidy's era, leaders could realize potential simply by working extremely hard and insisting that their people do the same, today's leaders, like Dillon, must foster specific attributes to achieve maximum success in themselves and their people. This book therefore focuses on those critical attributes—in particular, three catalysts—that leaders must harness in today's constantly challenging world if they hope to realize potential.

The Three Catalysts for Realizing Potential

First, let's dive more deeply into the idea of realizing potential. Far from a vague notion, *realizing potential* means rising to ever higher levels of achievement to the best of your abilities.

My research turned up three essential capabilities that allow leaders in today's turbulent world not only to perform at their best, but also to get the best out of their people. These drivers literally set in motion this fundamental function of leadership, and together they comprise the mental architecture we must develop in ourselves to be effective leaders. Each of these three traits is a catalyst of the mastery displayed by the most successful CEOs I found in my study, and I will briefly describe these catalysts here:

Realistic optimism: people with this trait possess confidence without self-delusion or irrationality. These people pursue audacious goals, which others would typically view as impossible pipedreams, while at the same time remaining aware of the magnitude of the challenges confronting them and the difficulties that lie ahead.

Subservience to purpose: people with this trait see their professional goal as so profound in importance that their lives become measured in value by how much they contribute to furthering that goal. What is more, they *must* be pursuing a professional goal in order to feel a purpose for living. In essence, that goal is their master and their reason for being. They do not ruminate about their purpose, because their mind finds satisfaction in its occupation with their goal. Their level of dedication to their work is a direct result of the extraordinary, remarkable importance they place on their goal.

Finding order in chaos: people with this ability find taking on multidimensional problems invigorating, and their ability to bring clarity to quandaries that baffle others makes their contributions invaluable.

Great leaders tap into each of these three abilities in a recursive, fluid way so that it isn't always easy to tease apart where one ability ends and another begins.

Beginning in chapter 2, I will define each of these catalysts in depth, including an examination of the subdrivers each contains. When I vet candidates for CEO positions in the country's top companies, I look for people who demonstrate *all three capabilities.* No organization should hire or promote into a leadership job someone who doesn't have the full suite of capabilities. They're a must-have for any aspiring leader.

The good news is that in most cases, *these three capabilities can be learned.* As I've hinted at before, people can change. By reading about the attributes of others, you can become aware of these critical attributes and choose to build them in yourself. While special training can also help, the interviews and exercises in this book offer an important starting point for that learning.

Just realizing your own potential, however, is not enough; you must also bring out the best in those you lead. Before we delve more deeply into the three catalysts, we'll look at the best way for leaders to do this—and why it is so important in today's world. Real leadership is what we call *recursive*: it's a continuous process that starts with a leader and is echoed in that leader's people. My research has shown that the best leaders work *with* the people they lead to seek their mutual maximum potential together: they cocreate their success. They don't do so randomly or chaotically; rather, they leverage identifiable organizing principles that we'll explore in this book. But it means that we can't just study leadership in a vacuum, since its very existence depends on this intimate, complex, and uniquely human interaction between people. Throughout this book, I share excerpts of my exchanges with relentless leaders. I attempt to demonstrate how they flip the critical switch of engagement in their people, the most positive and valuable outcome of the core evolution that is realizing potential.

Because an individual's own potential can only be realized through his or her work with others, success is created through a kind of recursive loop. This repeating process that drives individuals to press for ever more challenging but meaningful achievements explains why people could never hope to do so alone.

Creating a Context in Which People Can Realize Their Potential

As we began to see in the example of David Dillon, leaders who embody realistic optimism, subservience to purpose, and the ability to find order in chaos can use these abilities to craft *contexts* in which they and others can realize potential. We are all born with an innate urge for triumph, but we are not born aware of this need or how to meet it. As a result, unfortunately, few of us ever do reach our ultimate potential. Leaders who understand this innate need are able to bring that urge to the fore to harness the utmost effort from individuals over long stretches of time. The gratification that all human beings experience when distinguishing themselves doing something that matters lends this method its power and efficacy. Therefore, though the leader is the catalyst for people's actions, the people themselves must be responsible for realizing their own potential.

But for leaders to bring out this urge for triumph, they must recognize one of most profound truths of human psychology: that *no person has a fixed identity*. There is no lazy or hardworking person, no one who is only brilliant or stupid, conscientious or sloppy. Anyone, at any given time, is capable of manifesting any of these attributes. We are constantly making choices that determine which attribute is dominant at a given moment. In fact, all of us—including the leaders we most revere—have within us a veritable "committee of selves." (See "Heroes and Their Committee of Selves.") When we as leaders create a context for our people to realize their potential, we are creating a virtuous cycle that elicits our people's best selves—the selves that induce the gratification we all feel when we overcome significant challenges and realize our potential.

It is up to a leader to create a work environment in which every employee can experience the deep satisfaction of triumphing in pursuit of a worthy goal. Leaders' most critical responsibility lies in helping their people flip the switch of engagement toward realizing their potential as human beings, all within the demanding business environment of the twenty-first century. This is how a leader creates an organization that harnesses the utmost effort and resiliency from employees throughout its ranks—the only kind of organization that can survive amid ever-escalating competition. But only the most skilled of leaders can make that happen within their workforce.

Let's look at an example of how a leader can create a context for realizing potential in a situation of intense duress, rather than directly ordering a person to do something. The story is actually a well-known tale from the Bible in which Jesus is confronted by an angry mob. The crowd throws a woman onto the ground in front of their teacher and shouts, "This woman has been taken in adultery, in the very act.

Heroes and Their Committee of Selves

To master the process of soliciting the best performance from their people, leaders must first understand one essential truth about human psychology: that every human being is capable of both mediocrity and greatness. We assume that there is one person in each body, but each of us is more like a committee whose members have been thrown together to do a job. Consider two of the most widely revered leaders in business—Peter Drucker and Jack Welch.

Drucker is globally regarded as one of the most sought-after minds in management science. But he wasn't always right. For example, in September 1929, just a few weeks before the stock-market crash that led to the Great Depression, he began his career by publishing an article explaining why the New York Stock Exchange could only go *up*. Two decades later, writing about emerging trends in the packaging industry, he based his commentary on statistical analyses that were wildly incorrect. Years later, he told a reporter that a soap bubble exists for precisely twenty-five seconds (nonsense). Largely ignored in the United States for the first half of his seventy-year career, he was forced to go to Asia to find corporations interested in paying for his counsel. It wasn't until his involvement in some of Japan's revolutionary management techniques became better known that his advice became increasingly sought within the United States. But he was not always the sage we have come to know him as today; his wise and thoughtful self is complemented by a self that perhaps made snap judgments or read the facts wrong. In the end, Drucker was successful because he brought his best self to the fore.

As CEO of one of the world's largest corporations for nearly twenty years, Jack Welch increased the market cap of General Electric thirtyfold. He was famous for spending the majority of his time developing his people into what was widely regarded as the finest team of executives in the world and in the process built a company that became almost universally known as a talent factory. He personally selected and groomed his successor to carry on this legacy. But he too had his failures. During the eight years after his retirement, the company's performance dropped precipitately—its market capitalization fell to 20 percent of what it was when he led the company. The talent factory Welch had so carefully put in place did not have staying power. Despite these later disappointments, Welch was without a doubt one of the most influential CEOs of the twentieth century; he too focused on realizing his potential and that of those around him, deliberately choosing through discipline and hard work to bring his best self to the fore.

These two examples show that we can lionize or demonize even our most revered heroes. Perhaps Peter Drucker and Jack Welch have sometimes themselves been guilty of encouraging our heroic views of them. For them, it must have been a relief to ultimately experience mass admiration after many decades of sweat, struggle, uncertainty, and at times very public and harsh criticism. There is no question that the lifelong accomplishments of both Welch and Drucker have had an extraordinary impact on business.

But these examples show that every accomplished individual is also very flawed—and we must understand this paradox if we are to recognize what enables leaders to win their hard-earned reputations. The human longing to believe in the infallible leader is very powerful. To be under the direction of infallibility eases our fears in an uncertain future. But there are no gods in business or any other field. It's something we may know rationally, but we must truly debunk our tendencies to categorize people as heroes or losers, gods or charlatans, and we must especially eliminate our penchant for categorizing and oversimplifying great leaders. They do not get it right every time—just much more often than their competitors, and for a much longer period. All good leaders have times of weakness, when their less heroic selves emerge. These are the sides of them that we do not celebrate and choose to forget when we build them into heroic caricatures. Knowing this will help all of us on our own quest to realize our potential and bring forth our best selves.

The law says she shall be stoned. What say you?" The group's lust for harsh justice is intense, an aggressive challenge to Jesus's core teaching that society needs to display more compassion.

It would be easy for Jesus to take this opportunity to preach to the crowd about the importance of empathy, understanding, or forgiveness. But in this moment, he needs another, more effective way to convince the people to put aside their anger and manifest their better selves. So he resists the urge, turns from the group as if he has not heard them, squats down in the sand, and begins to simply doodle. The crowd continues to shout, exhorting him to give an answer about what to do. After a few minutes, he stands and utters a phrase that has been quoted through the ages: "Let he who is without sin among you, let him be the first to cast a stone at her." Then Jesus squats back down and continues doodling.

The crowd is silent for a few moments as the people wrestle with identifying who among them can begin the stoning. And then one by one, they walk away, chastened by their own lack of purity and how it interfered with their entitlement to righteous condemnation. While Jesus's words are famously repeated in exhortations to us all to enact precisely this type of kind humility, I see the real brilliance here in the way that his words force the people in the mob to come to their *own* conclusions. They are responsible for the choice. Jesus is not telling them what to do; he is not telling them to condemn the woman. Neither is he telling them to stop—rather, he helps each person there to realize his or her own potential to make the most humane decision. In that way, by making the decision themselves, the people experience their higher selves.

By throwing out a question and then silently turning to his own activities, doodling in the sand, Jesus quietly creates a *context* in which his followers can internalize the importance of his mission to increase compassion in human society. This is much more effective than his other options because it makes the mob decide. And because the people have now experienced their higher selves, the incident affects how they will act in similar situations in the future.

So how does this quiet context-setting translate into today's business world? In a more contemporary example, David Novak, CEO of Yum! Brands, shared one example of how he created a context for himself and his people to cocreate success. He described his visit to the company's Fort Apache, Baltimore, location, which was struggling:

> Pride is the greatest human motivator. People want to go to work feeling part of something great. But the people in that Baltimore plant, they knew they were a part of something less than mediocrity. They knew that they were absolutely not doing anything great. And they were blaming everybody else and suffered from a severe case of victimitis.
>
> And all I did was tap into [that] fact . . . I said, "Hey, you've identified a lot of big issues that need to be solved. And you

have a lot of good ideas. You've been in this business for fifteen years. You know I'm not going to fix this. I got to go back to [the corporate office]. So if things are going to get better, it's up to you to fix this. The only thing I'm going to do is come back later to see how great you can be when you set your mind to it. I'm coming back to see what you've been able to do." And then it was like I took their excuses away.[4]

Not long afterward, the Baltimore plant fixed its performance problems, and Novak didn't have to fire anyone.

How could Novak trust that his people would change the way that they were working? "I think people want to go to work with a quest towards greatness," he told me. By turning the table on them and tapping into that pride—that quest—he engaged them in a way that direct orders or reprimands wouldn't have done. Instead, under Novak's leadership, the company is focused on training in the whole organization. "Secretaries, admins, VPs, they're all going through it," Novak said. "This is a demonstration that everyone counts, regardless of the level you are at in the company. We're *all* a part of something special, achieving greatness."

The best leaders can tap into the universal human thirst for pride and self-improvement, no matter what industry they are in and regardless of the content of their organization's mission statement. They do this in many ways. Herb Kelleher, founder and former CEO of Southwest Airlines, made a lot of self-deprecating jokes when I spoke with him. He argued that humility and nonhierarchical thinking play a big role in realizing the potential of a workforce:

Humility is a very important ingredient for an effective, strong CEO. And if you have that sense of humbleness, you'll feel perfectly happy making jokes about yourself because you understand your own inadequacies, you understand how other people can help you enormously in areas where you need help, and you can have enormous fun with everybody that works for you because you're all the same. You're not members of different classes. So it's always easy to be humble when you have lots to be humble about.[5]

For example, Kelleher turned organizational hierarchy upside down at Southwest Airlines. One vice president even came to his office to complain that he didn't see Kelleher as much as the baggage handlers saw him. "An organization chart shouldn't dictate what you do," Kelleher told me. "I have always preached that the general office is just there to support the people in the field, the people in the trenches that are doing the fighting every day."

This lack of hierarchy at Southwest Airlines allowed him to cocreate success with his people at a company where, according to every productivity metric, the employees work harder than their peers at competing airlines. "If you like your job," Kelleher said, "you do tend to work harder at it, to show up for work more often. We do this by getting out of people's way. We say, 'We're going to give you the latitude to handle customers on the spot, give you the flexibility to deal with them because frankly, we're too stupid in the general office to know what to do with a hundred million encounters a year. So we'll leave it up to you.' And, of course, that makes people understand that they're an important part of things, that they're being trusted to make those kinds of decisions every day."

Yet Kelleher has taken this kind of servant leadership one step further: "We also give employees the opportunity to grow in what they do at Southwest Airlines. We don't typecast them and say, 'Well, gee, you joined us as a ramp agent, so I guess you're going to work on the ramp for the rest of your life.' We move people around; we look for their stroke of genius, their inspiration, and say, 'Hey, wait a second. We've got something over here that might be more rewarding for you in terms of keeping your interest.'"

Almost every human being alive today has an underutilized thirst for bettering himself or herself. It is up to leaders to discover how to trigger this thirst—in fact, it is a leader's most critical responsibility. Doing so is challenging enough in an environment that allows for calm reflection, but today's business world is more like the angry mob that surrounded Jesus. It is one of intense, ongoing stress, and ever-increasing complexity.

Life at the Wheel in a Global Economy

Globalization has exponentially increased the complexity and pressure under which today's leaders must perform. But leaders who know how to realize potential actually perform best under fire. These relentless leaders, when confronted with sustained levels of stress and complexity, become hypereffective. In a sense, they have come to master their reaction to stress in a way that turns it into a high-octane fuel that allows them to operate with peak efficiency.

Take, for example, Andrea Jung, who was named chair and CEO of Avon in 1999. At the time, the 120-year-old company was in danger of collapse. Its brand image had grown stale, and its market share was dropping at an alarming rate. Although she had never been a CEO, Jung accepted the challenge and began to remake the company and its image. By 2002, she had led the company to a phase of torrid growth, and her accomplishments marked her as one of the most celebrated CEOs in the world.

But in 2005, dramatic, unexpected shifts in the global cosmetics market placed the company in peril once again. In a conversation in

May 2008, she described what it was like to lead through a severe downturn after a period of extraordinary growth: "During times like that, the decisions I have to make are hard to bear. At times I questioned whether I had the stomach to make them. But now looking back, I realize this period was one of the most important learning experiences of my life."[6]

Jung told me how shifts in the global market required her to cut costs by more than $300 million, which meant laying off a lot of people she had personally recruited. What's more, industry analysts criticized how she decided to use the savings brought about by this restructuring: to enter the Chinese market and increase Avon's overall advertising budgets—rather than using the money to prop up the company's depressed share values.

"It's true that these moves hurt our numbers in the short term, but they were the right moves to keep us growing and competitive," she said. "We also decided to suspend announcements of Avon's earnings projections. Unpopular but necessary. We needed to get our focus away from meeting quarterly earnings targets and back to growing and sustaining the company over the long term."

Jung's actions at Avon illustrate one of the three catalysts of realizing potential in yourself and your people: *subservience to purpose.* Rather than doing what was expected, Jung found the inner fortitude to ignore the prevailing wisdom—and bad press—and follow through on a plan to secure the company's long-term success. By 2007, Jung's controversial turnaround plan was vindicated as Avon's stock price reached a 40 percent premium over its 2005 low. And once again, the same business press that had begun questioning her competence was now lauding Andrea Jung. Her experience with the volatility of doing business in the twenty-first century illustrates the new normal surrounding leadership—and what it takes to maximize potential and excel in this environment. Unfortunately, few individuals find themselves prepared to take the helm under these conditions, and as a result, otherwise very talented senior executives buckle under the pressure.

When Leading Under Pressure
Doesn't Yield Success

Realizing potential under the kinds of conditions leaders face today demands developing critical attributes (realistic optimism, subservience to purpose, and the ability to find order in chaos) that I briefly defined earlier and that this book will explore in detail. When people lacking these abilities are placed in charge of organizations, not only are they *not* up to the challenge of the new world environment, but they also can cause extraordinary damage.

For example, in chapter 2, we will look at the case of "Tom," a candidate for CEO at an insurance company.[7] The board asked me to find out why, despite his outstanding qualifications on paper, Tom had been passed over for the top position at his previous company. I found that both at his old company and in our interviews, he showed little or no awareness of actual circumstances about *himself*. His acute inability to look at his own behavior rendered him a serious liability in a CEO job in today's market. Similarly, "Craig," a CEO at a utility company (chapter 4), demonstrated a complete lack of subservience to purpose, despite being well liked by his people. His need to avoid conflict at any cost destroyed his effectiveness as the company's leader.

The challenge of leading under pressure also bested "Gary," CEO of one of America's oldest metals companies. But in 2006, the company had to be auctioned for private sale after spiraling into a state of rapid decay.

Gary, who had degrees from Harvard and MIT, joined an elite management consulting company in the late 1970s. His success in client services led to quick promotions up the firm's hierarchy, eventually landing him in charge of the logistics and distribution practice.

That's where, in the early 1990s, the metals company's CEO, "Mark," met Gary and was immediately impressed with his extraordinary intellectual horsepower and ideas for how to transform the highly conservative metals business. When Mark retired in 1994, he named Gary the next CEO.

But despite his obvious intelligence, Gary's response to the pressure and complexity of the job caused him to act in ways that were highly unresponsive to the realities of the steel business. His difficulties coping with the magnitude of the CEO role, coupled with an overly accommodating board, allowed the company to languish through a decade of subpar performance.

Gary's inflexibility was a key flaw. As one former colleague put it, "Prior to becoming CEO, Gary was known for his masterful strategic-thinking skills. He was top-notch. But as CEO, he conceived horribly flawed strategies and was unwilling to reconsider them when they clearly weren't working."

For instance, the commodities market had always experienced dramatic cycles of both boom and bust. But as the twentieth century came to a close, these cycles were occurring with more frequency and complexity. Gary felt that it was critical to make the company's revenue base more stable in the hopes that the firm would become more immune to these cycles. He instituted an elite-customer program, which directed the field offices to focus their energy on their highest-volume buyers, such as Caterpillar and John Deere, which were willing to sign long-term deals that locked in fixed prices. To force his regions to comply with his strategy of retaining only the largest customers, Gary sent out letters to all his smaller customers, explaining that the company would no longer be able to service their needs. In Gary's mind, he was going to take a workforce that had become accustomed to a fluctuating marketplace and force it into a business model that maximized stability.

But the metal industry's fluidity was not going to change, and success within it required an entrepreneurial approach that Gary continued to eschew, even when this blind spot was pointed out to him. One former employee recollected, "I got a call from an appliance manufacturer that was introducing a new product line and needed a particular kind of metal delivered quickly. Speed and responsiveness was their concern, not price. There was a ton of high-margin work that would pop up around the country like this. But under Gary's new guidelines, we were unable to respond to these opportunities, and he resisted any efforts that deviated from his plan."

A man who had always been known for his prodigious intellect and exceptional strategic thinking was unable to react quickly to the multiple pressures of market changes and customer demands. He stubbornly pursued a strategy that was clearly not working, a sign that he was woefully inadequate when it came to finding order in chaos. The pressure of the circumstances was overwhelming a mind that was historically capable of brilliant analytic instincts. Gary's company quickly began to be outmaneuvered by the number two metals company, whose CEO allowed the regional offices a high degree of independence to meet changes in local demands.

As the metals market's dramatic acceleration between boom and bust intensified, Gary's company, now locked into large, long-term contracts with its buyers, could not take advantage of increases in prices during the boom times. With the company's performance continuing to languish, Gary blamed his mistakes on others, demonstrating his severe lack of realistic optimism by failing to recognize how his own behaviors were aggravating the crisis. For instance, whenever the failure of his initiatives was pointed out to him, he deflected responsibility and insisted that the company's "club" of longtime insiders was simply out to get him by refusing to implement his ideas. To be fair, many of his regional offices were indeed disregarding his orders, but their disobedience was due to Gary's refusal to listen to their very relevant concerns and not, as he perceived, their irrational reaction to having to report to someone they considered an outsider.

He did nothing to reverse his eroded authority and simply continued to blame the "clublike" attitude of metal industry employees and their unwillingness to follow the directions of an outsider. Ultimately, all of these moves exposed Gary's inability to realize the potential of either himself or his workforce.

Yet Gary proceeded as if nothing was wrong. For ten years, the company lurched from one unsuccessful initiative to another. Finally, in 2007, its net income dropped 27 percent to $71.8 million on sales of $5.9 billion, while the company's closest competitor grew its earnings by 73 percent, to $354.5 million on sales of $5.7 billion. These numbers forced a rebellion among shareholders, and Gary's company was auctioned off to a private-equity firm, which promptly fired him.

Gary looked as though he had it all as a potential CEO: smarts, ideas, and a deep understanding of business. But he struggled in the CEO role because he lacked the critical attributes required to manifest the maximum potential of his people in today's business environment. He is not the only one: the absence of these attributes represents a common denominator in many of the underperforming CEOs I've evaluated, as I will illustrate in examples throughout this book.

Methodology and Research

My research for this book is based on two primary sources. First, my colleagues and I gathered performance data for approximately two hundred candidates being assessed for the role of CEO at major U.S.

corporations. These assessments included cognitive-ability testing, behavioral interviewing, and peer performance ratings (this data included a normal distribution of executives possessing differing talent levels, from a wide variety of companies). Second, I conducted psychological interviews between 2006 and 2010 with just over sixty current and retired CEOs from the world's largest companies, as described below.

Why the focus on CEOs and not other types of leaders? First, CEOs are an incredibly valuable source of information about what works and what doesn't in a high-pressure business leadership role. And second, this book is intended primarily for those of you who aspire to exactly these kinds of positions of corporate and business leadership. It is my goal that the voices of these great leaders will set the context for you to realize your own potential as a leader.

How did we determine the key behavioral traits of the most effective leaders from this raw data? First we classified the two hundred candidates in our database into three groups, with the top-performing quartile labeled "highly successful," the middle two quartiles characterized as "average performers," and the bottom quartile as "highly ineffective." The behaviors of the top-performing quartile were then compared with those of the bottom by means of a behavioral analysis. We grouped together into categories similar behaviors or attributes that had been identified as being prominent in each test subject. These behaviors were cited as being largely responsible for the execution success or failure of each individual. We then analyzed those groupings to identify the underlying psychological construct that best defined the overall category.

What emerged was startling. Six critical attributes were highly consistent within the top performers, regardless of industry or job type. Clearly, this mental architecture was responsible for the execution ability of the most effective executives operating under duress. What is more, these attributes were almost totally absent among the bottom performing quartile. Further analysis revealed that these six attributes could be sorted into three meta-attributes, or what I call catalysts earlier in this introduction: realistic optimism, subservience to purpose, and finding order in chaos.

I then set out to conduct psychological interviews with around sixty current and retired CEOs (average tenure in CEO role was nine years) to help clarify the role each of these factors played in their leadership. Of these, I included in this book twenty-five representative CEO interviews (in alphabetical order):

Gordon Bethune, chairman and CEO (retired), Continental Airlines

Larry Bossidy, chairman and CEO (retired), Honeywell, Inc.

Ron Daniel, managing partner (retired), McKinsey & Company

Marijn Dekkers, chairman and CEO, Thermo Fisher

David Dillon, chairman and CEO, The Kroger Co.

Fred Hassan, chairman and CEO, Schering-Plough

Andrea Jung, chairman and CEO, Avon Products, Inc.

Herb Kelleher, founder and CEO (retired), Southwest Airlines

Dick Keyser, chairman and CEO, W.W. Grainger, Inc.

James Kilts, chairman and CEO (retired), The Gillette Company

A. G. Lafley, chairman and CEO, Procter & Gamble

Ralph Larsen, chairman and CEO (retired), Johnson & Johnson

Richard Lenny, chairman and CEO (retired), The Hershey Company

Ray Milchovich, chairman and CEO, Foster Wheeler

James McNulty, chairman and CEO (retired), Parsons Corporation

David Novak, chairman and CEO, Yum! Brands

Jim Skinner, Vice Chairman and CEO, McDonald's Corporation

Dave O'Reilly, chairman and CEO, Chevron Corporation

Fred Smith, chairman and CEO, Federal Express

James Owens, chairman and CEO, Caterpillar Inc.

Joe Swedish, chairman and CEO, Trinity Health Systems

Irene Rosenfeld, chairman and CEO, Kraft Foods Inc.

Chris Van Gorder, chairman and CEO, Scripps Health System

Kevin Sharer, chairman and CEO, Amgen Inc.

Miles White, chairman and CEO, Abbott Laboratories

I began the interviews in 2006 and completed the bulk of them in 2008 and 2009. Each interview lasted a minimum of sixty minutes, but most lasted several hours, sometimes spread out over two to three separate sessions. Most were done in person at the CEO's office, where I conducted an in-depth psychological interview about the leader's past and his or her accomplishments, failures, fears, and moments of pride.

One core conclusion emerged: the best CEOs had been, and continued to be, distinguished by their ability to manifest the very best from their workforce. Yet in my interviews with the CEOs, it became clear that the three attributes that allowed them to do so had become even more important by the beginning of the twenty-first century.

It's Not So Simple

In my job assessing candidates for CEO positions, I am continuously pressed by boards of directors to comply with a "reductionist" model of explaining human behavior, in which I'm asked to break issues down into component parts that can then be isolated and measured. When I walk into a board room to discuss the CEO candidates that I am assessing, the board usually asks me essentially to "categorize this person—is the candidate an A, a B, or a C?"

But inevitably, the answer is more complicated than that, and I find myself having to broaden the discussion to involve the context of the company, the job, and the team that is to be managed and how each individual's unique qualities would likely influence future outcomes. Nevertheless, as I began writing this book, I found myself falling into the same reductionist trap that my clients so often did. I was trying to reduce human behavior into a linear progression, a unidirectional model of success: "Develop attributes A, B, and C, and you too can be successful." The temptation of offering an easy solution for the reader is strong. But this overly simplistic assessment just isn't right, and it doesn't honor the very spirit of what I've found out about great leaders.

Such reductionism doesn't work, because these three attributes are a *symptom* of the mastery these CEOs displayed, as much as they are a cause. In other words, as much as these qualities did indeed differentiate the successful leaders from unsuccessful ones, the attributes are not ends in and of themselves. Rather, they are parts of a much larger whole—the whole of leaders who realize the potential of themselves and of their people. This fundamental point ties all of these people together in a way that defines their greatness. It is something they had discovered unconsciously, individually, and it has made them great.

The Value of the Real Thing

Honoring this complexity has influenced the way this book is written and conceived. The real words of the interviews are brought front and center so that they themselves can create the very real context for readers to realize their own potential. The value of the insights provided by these CEOs is best internalized and understood when we experience the leaders' own words. Their real-life experiences help us understand what it means to be a great leader. To truly understand and gain from their wisdom, we must immerse ourselves in their psychology and witness the recurring patterns of how they organize their worldview. Although I have organized the book in a way that, I hope, best illuminates these patterns, I also encourage you to decide for yourself what is going on.

Herb Kelleher, the aforementioned founder and retired CEO of Southwest Airlines, used to run a periodic event called "corporate days," which drew people from companies around the world. Kelleher recalled that the visitors would ask things like "How do you hire? How do you train? How do you motivate? How do you keep morale up?"[8] And most of them left somewhat discouraged when he explained that Southwest Airlines didn't have some magic formula or perfect model, any more than there is a perfect model for raising a family. "We told people that it's got to come from your heart, not your head, to be effective," Kelleher says, "that it's a feeling of empathy towards your people and of acting out of their best interests. If your people feel that you truly have their best interests in mind, they'll give you their best. And you do that by creating a system that gives them the freedom to grow, to play an important role, and to be part of something great."

The reason Southwest Airlines' visitors had such a hard time replicating this model was because they were looking for a list of practices. They wanted to analyze the system, break down its component parts, isolate what made Southwest Airlines unique from other airlines, and then replicate those practices in their own system. In trying to use reductionist thinking on a complex system, they were destroying the core principles that made the Southwest Airlines model so potent in the first place.

So here, as was the case at Southwest Airlines, we have a unique opportunity and challenge: to explore the topic of leadership without resorting to reductionist buckets and categories, but still learning about the key characteristics that are critical to greatness in the field. In chapter 1, we will explore more deeply the core-driving principle of realizing potential. Chapters 2 through 7 will detail the components of the three catalysts we need to realize our potential in a fast-paced world. The book concludes in chapter 8 with an example in which one leader illustrates how all three drivers are leveraged toward realizing the potential of a workforce.

So now let's begin this recursive journey together. We will start with an in-depth exploration of the phenomenon of realizing potential, with all of its nuances.

1

Learning How to Realize Potential

The best leaders solicit the best possible performance from themselves and from their people amid the constant change and duress that define enterprise today. Although we are all born with a drive to realize our potential (as I will describe later in this chapter), the *ability* to realize that potential requires deeply personal experiences that enable it to emerge. Each time we feel its fruition, we become more aware of its power and the factors required to make it happen. Yet realizing our potential always involves the ongoing, disciplined pursuit of doing something that matters. Regardless of the stage of life in which you first realize your potential, it is always deeply rewarding. But the great leaders in this book learned how to master it relatively early in their lives and later used it to build high-performing, highly adaptive organizations.

In this chapter, we will look first at an example of one such leader whose ability to realize potential became a lifelong practice. Then we will explore how realizing our individual potential is actually an innate drive and a thirst we have as human beings. Finally, we will explore how great leaders tap into and gratify that lifelong thirst for betterment and learning by making the increasingly demanding competitive market tangible for their employees. I will show how the never-ending competition for survival that underlies capitalism is not unlike the fight for survival ingrained in every organism.

Realizing Potential: A Lifelong Process

Fred Hassan, CEO of Schering-Plough, is well known for his abilities as a turnaround specialist and is a stellar leader in the twenty-first-century economy. His story exemplifies many of the key elements of a life lived in the pursuit of fulfilling potential in himself and others. That story begins in childhood; Hassan told me that it was his upbringing in Pakistan that originally taught him that dedication to improving yourself could lead to success and fulfillment.[1] There, he watched and learned as his father, a civil servant, never failed to fulfill his duty even under the most trying circumstances. "I remember when I was very young, there was a horrible flood," he said, "and as soon as my father received the news, he left to go help. He was concerned about snake bites because so many [snakes] come out during floods. So he worked hard to access as much anti-snake-bite serum as possible and then personally showed up in the flooded areas to lead relief efforts. He did not hesitate to go."

And it was there that his mother modeled a similar lesson of courage as a prominent activist for women's rights in a region where such ideas were unheard-of. One of the most important fruits of her influence over young Fred was to teach him to overcome his speech impediment. "The term for it in stutterer's language is circumlocution," he told me. "Stutterers tend to go around the words that give them trouble, avoiding them as much as possible. My mom taught me that the more you do that, the more conscious you become of your struggle, which in turn makes the stutter even worse. So what she pushed me to do was to gain the strength and confidence to push through those tough syllables. It's not easy, but I worked hard at it, and while I'm not a hundred percent cured, I'm so functional now that people often express surprise when they hear about my past challenges with stuttering."

And finally, it was in Pakistan, too, that Hassan benefited from an influential teacher who pushed him into taking the entrance exams for engineering school, at a time when Hassan had decided the exams would be too hard. He recounted: "I was the first in my family to go deeply into science and math. My older brother had left this area and opted for liberal arts, but my physics teacher refused to hear that from me. He said he knew I could do it. And just his saying that kept me going." In the end, Hassan did quite well on the exams, even earning a full scholarship to the best engineering school in Europe.

Fred Hassan was fortunate enough to have people in his life who took an express interest in teaching him about the innate gratification derived from hard work. Once he had experienced that gratification, Hassan's thirst for ever-more-significant challenges became like a flywheel, feeding on its own momentum. In his career, he has actively sought out the most difficult corporate assignments, including turnarounds at companies like Pharmacia and Schering-Plough. Having internalized realizing his own potential, he now had the tools to teach these lessons to others, and these tools quickly became the cornerstone of his leadership approach.

"I don't just demand things of people," Hassan told me. "You have to make them want to do it, and the best way is to paint the picture of what we're trying to do, and hope that they can buy into the picture." Schering-Plough, for example, faced almost insurmountable manufacturing problems. While most conventional leaders would have focused just on pleasing the U.S. Food and Drug Administration (FDA) and other regulators, Hassan took a different approach.

He told his people, "This is not about getting out of trouble. It's about becoming good on the inside when it comes to process excellence, quality systems, a management attitude of improving all the time." And not only did the company get out of trouble, but it actually "became a very strong, sustainable, quality-driven organization, not only in manufacturing but also in other areas."

One thing Hassan did to turn Schering around was to move the sales force's compensation system from 60/40 salary-versus-commission split to an 80/20 split. When he made this announcement, he got a standing ovation, even from the salespeople who would be making less. You would think this audience would be more money-driven, but it wasn't. "And I also told them something else," Hassan said. "When it comes to choosing between making a sale and doing what's right, that they should walk away if that's what's right. When people hear their leader standing there who absolutely tells them to lose a sale if they're going to feel good about it because they didn't do anything inappropriate, they feel very secure with that thing. That's why they stood up and applauded. They were looking for that comfort, because on the inside, people want to do the right thing." Hassan asserted that realizing your potential is less about making more money, and more about a deeper mission to become the best person you can be.

"I think overall, if you were to characterize me and the people who work for me," Hassan continued, "I lose very, very few people, particularly 'A' players. This is something I'm very proud of, because probably for the first time in their lives, these people really want to be part of the team. They actually enjoy coming to work, and of course, money is always there as a factor, but it's not the driving force."

Hassan made it his primary mission to teach his people the gratification that comes from doing challenging, purposeful work. His childhood experiences with his parents and teachers showed him that a thirst for meaningful, hard work had to be taught, but that once exposed to it, people come to internalize it as a powerful, motivating force.

As a good leader, you must keep this idea front and center, even when making a decision that seems to have nothing to do with your employees. When Hassan had to address Schering-Plough's FDA violations, he did not simply correct the cited incidents. Instead, he embarked on changing the whole organizational culture to one that focused on putting forth excellence in every aspect of the business. By doing so, the production facility problems that led to the FDA sanctions in the first place disappeared. Hassan's approach understood that the problem was not any particular person or sloppy procedures, but that individuals in the culture had not yet been taught that achieving excellence was the only path to achieving a gratifying life. Hassan was not simply preaching "mission-based" leadership that he learned from a textbook. Great leaders can only hope to influence today's highly sophisticated workforce through authenticity. Hassan fixed the cause of the problem, and the problem itself went away.

Hassan's sincere commitment to the role of realizing potential as the cornerstone for a lifetime of overall satisfaction has continued. At age sixty-two, he talked about looking for his next opportunity. "I don't know clearly what I'll be doing yet, now that we are merging with Merck. I do get a lot of opportunities that come to me, but my whole approach is that it has to feel great in your own heart and then you grab it and give everything you can to it."

Most important, Hassan said, he won't allow fear to drive his own decision making. The only thing he truly fears, he said, is complacency: "I like to look upon work as a social system and seeing people do well around me and people grow. That gives me enormous satisfaction wherever I go. Complacency is the enemy of making this happen."

Retirement had no appeal for Hassan, because that would mean walking away from his life's pursuit of helping others to constantly improve and make meaningful contributions. Retirement would take away the very experiences that gave his life a profound sense of purpose. Fred Hassan was fortunate to have people in his childhood who taught him how to realize potential, an advantage that placed him well ahead of his peer group in his readiness to lead others at a young age. By personally experiencing the gratification that comes from triumph in the pursuit of meaningful achievements, he instinctively began creating environments that would do the same for his employees. As a result, Hassan embarked on a forty-year career of relentless leadership, turning underperforming groups like Schering-Plough into best-in-class operations.

But the internalizing of an ethic that pursues ever-higher achievement is not simply a job. It represents a value system that permeates every aspect of life. It is the surest way for you to reach a sense of satisfaction that your life has made a difference and that, in getting up in the morning, you have a strong sense of meaningful purpose with which to spend your time. To be needed, and valuable, is a fundamental human longing that never fades, regardless of life stage.

Thus we find that relentless leaders who fully realize their potential never stop pursuing new challenges and opportunities. And in so doing, they have learned to first recognize and then satisfy an urge that has been with them since birth.

Satisfying Our Innate Thirst for Realizing Potential

Where does this urge come from?

The year is 1946, and Jean Piaget, the man who would become the father of developmental psychology, is going through his day as another kind of father—to the colicky three-month-old Lucienne. To distract his daughter and calm her incessant crying, Piaget hung a colorful mobile above her crib. For a few days, whenever Piaget wanted to soothe his daughter, he would give the mobile a spin, and Lucienne would stare up at the pretty new object and giggle. But after a week, Lucienne's indigestion made her fussy and restless again, and the spinning mobile rendered no effect.

That is when Piaget tied a ribbon from Lucienne's toe to a piece of the mobile. Lucienne's reaction was immediate as she let out a slew of excited giggles. Piaget had never before heard such an intense reaction from her. Over the coming days, Piaget noticed entirely new expressions on Lucienne's face. She was focused, concentrating, trying to control the foot tied to the mobile. As soon as she had realized that by controlling her foot she could control the movement of the mobile, she became determined to master the movements of both. Whenever Piaget untied the string, Lucienne protested vigorously. Upon mastering each new set of movements, she was ecstatic. Her excitement over this accomplishment, however, lasted only a few days before she grew bored of the activity and turned her attention to new challenges she had yet to master.

As Piaget observed, the innate need for new achievements is present in every child. But to *recognize and develop* that drive and use it toward realizing potential is something that must be learned. Moreover, this natural drive for realizing potential often becomes thwarted by the vagaries of daily life—the never-ending in-box; the fatigue of an unfocused, harried day; or the numbness of repeated failures. Certainly the expression of this eager drive wanes for most people as they mature and experience competing impulses. For instance, the urge to master the act of scaling a tall tree inevitably comes up against the memory of the pain that follows a bad fall. In this sense, our drive to realize our potential comes up against our committee of selves holding us back and working at cross-purposes.

For most people, the risks associated with any situation dominate their attention. From an evolutionary standpoint, this makes complete sense. If you were designing the mind of a fish, you would not have it respond as strongly to opportunities as to threats, since the cost of missing a sign of a nearby predator could be catastrophic. This principle is called *negativity bias*. Human minds react to bad things more quickly, strongly, and persistently than to equivalent good things. As a result, once children grow into adulthood, their behavior tends toward avoidance, designed to minimize confrontations with risk, danger, or other unpleasantness.

This is why the urge to unwind—to curl up comfortably on the sofa whenever we can get away with it—is so strong.[2] Because this conservative urge is so powerful, most people take any opportunity to wind down and park the mind in neutral. Individuals tend to be more immediately drawn to the comfort of relaxation rather than to the challenge of discovery. For most adults, their shadow selves—rife with fear, shame, and a sense of inadequacy—prevent them from taking on significant challenges. They instead choose to engage in less threatening pursuits.

But by succumbing to this impulse, they inevitably feel restless and less than proud of themselves. If you as a leader can help your people rediscover and fulfill their own innate need to master new accomplishment, you have realized an enormous opportunity, one that will be critical for all leaders to master in order to survive in today's world.

One of the great all-time fallacies is that human beings want to balance their lives with an equal proportion of work and leisure. On the contrary, the happiest and most satisfied people tend to spend the majority of their time and energy in effortful activities, not leisure. This is because self-esteem can only be generated by distinguishing yourself through purposeful work. This is a critical point for leaders to recognize—about themselves *and* about the people they lead.

When you believe strongly in the importance of your enterprise, there is nothing you'd rather do than pursue it. By experiencing your own critical role in pushing forward something meaningful, you feel important. Thus begins the virtuous cycle of working so hard that you gain distinction, which gives you the pleasure derived from a sense that you matter, which in turn causes you to rededicate yourself to working hard. You cannot be a great leader without understanding the importance of teaching the deep gratification that can only be attained through discipline. It is an essential component to helping others manifest their potential for great achievement.

This virtuous cycle holds on a much larger scale as well. The beauty of capitalism is that it is extremely well suited for creating a system that taps into this human truth. The cyclical nature of the innate quest for human achievement helps explain why capitalism has created an unprecedented level of prosperity in the societies that practice it. Capitalism has no finish line. Within this system is replicated a never-ending competition for survival that is not unlike the fight for survival ingrained in every organism. As a result, competing organizations have an innate desire for continuous improvement. They must continually strive to improve if they are to survive, and this continual improvement and growth spurs them to seek even more.

The Role of Competing Impulses in Realizing Potential

Let's return for a moment to Piaget's baby daughter, Lucienne. Her fascination with making the mobile spin led Piaget to draw conclusions about our innate drive as human beings—to master what we're capable of mastering, to reach for our full potential, a thirst that can't be sated. But often this impulse is in direct competition with other obligations, wants, or expectations. For example, as we think of retirement, we may find that continually reaching for new goals is hard to give up, as Fred Hassan described earlier in this chapter. Or, we may want to rest, spend more time on hobbies and with our families, while at the same time feeling this drive toward accomplishment. The not-so-subtle tug of distinctly competing impulses is that committee of selves at war within us. How do great leaders make sense of this struggle?

Many great leaders demonstrate a subservience to a single purpose that guides them through life, as we will discuss in chapters 4 and 5; however, the struggle that leads to this unilateral approach bears scrutiny as well. Many CEOs I work with are entering a new stage of their professional lives. They have served their companies for long tenures and are preparing to announce their successor. It's why they contact me in the first place. After they step down, they continue to lead very busy lives, serving on boards, teaching, writing, and acting as advisers. For nearly all, a part of them feels restless, misses being at the heart of a great undertaking. Still, most are not so compelled as to take on the massive commitment required to be CEO again. They have entered a different phase in their life in which their main impulse is to pursue a broader variety of activities and reduced levels of work. They retire on their own terms, and while it doesn't lead to an endless feeling of bliss, the decision is right for them.

"Rick" was not at this stage. When I was introduced to Rick six years into his first CEO job, he was hitting it out of the park. For the ten years before earning his first CEO role, he had reported to one of the greatest CEOs of the twentieth century. Upon leaving that organization and taking over a troubled company, he masterfully turned it around. The business press widely recognized him as one of the up-and-coming leaders in his industry. Then, an unusual set of circumstances caused Rick, at only age fifty-three, to leave the company, and he found himself in a situation that had forced him to step down before he was really ready to move on—and it showed.

Over the years, I had always found Rick to be exceptionally personable and perceptive, which is why I often contact him to talk about my research ideas. He invariably challenges my notions and pushes my thinking. This day was no different, as he listened to my update on what I'd found and he jumped in to pick certain conclusions apart. But the tone and cadence with which he was speaking was noticeably agitated, even aggressive.

Curious about the obvious shift in his energy, I asked him what he was doing with his time in the few months since he'd stepped down as CEO. He'd moved back to his home town to be closer to his family, and he explained that he was busier than ever teaching classes at a nearby business school and advising several boards. Rick talked about how great it was to spend more time doing things that he never had the time to do as CEO. But his tone was edgy, particularly as he talked about the current economic collapse and how the CEO opportunities that had come his way thus far were not inspiring. He sounded like a caged tiger.

Rick was so edgy because he longed to put to work the vast array of skills he had spent a lifetime building. Teaching, serving on boards, and spending more time with family was special to him. But he even more profoundly longed for the challenge and gratification of taking a large organization and making it into a top-performing one.

To repeat the idea discussed in the introduction, we are all a committee of selves. All great leaders inevitably struggle with impossible choices if they are to realize the potential in themselves and their people. Every relentless leader I've ever interviewed has talked with tremendous satisfaction about his or her life's work, about the gratitude felt in having had the opportunity to make a difference in the lives of so many. But when the subject turns to families, the amount of time spent on the road away from home, the person's eyes inevitably soften and the tone shifts. There is no perfect life, no way to be two places at once. There is no great leader I know that wouldn't have loved to spend more time at home with his or her family—not one that doesn't regret having to miss a share of important experiences with his or her children or spouse.

But this is one of the unavoidable truths of being alive. We are all rife with competing impulses, but the simple fact remains that you cannot be two places at once. You cannot both go to the Olympics and attend your senior prom. You cannot live two lives and then look back at both and choose which one you liked better. The subject of this book, realizing potential, is addressing how we human beings enable ourselves and others to attain deep, long-term gratification—to achieve a life that makes us feel that we matter—that our existence has made a profound, positive difference in the world. But this is not to suggest that doing so means that you will have it all, that you will avoid the inevitable regret that accompanies choices made. Realizing your potential means making those choices, and regret is realistically a natural, inevitable part of that process.

And yet just because realizing potential involves an extraordinary level of dedication, it does not mean one forgoes all other meaningful activities. In fact, great leaders know that they must maintain a healthy personal life during this pursuit if they are to be truly relentless leaders.

Ralph Larsen, CEO of Johnson & Johnson (retired), spoke about the importance of balance for all true leaders:

> I think it is very important for a leader, whether it's a CEO or other leader, to work on his family life. If you've got chaos in your home, you can't do this job. You just can't. So you've got to make sure that you have the right balance between your work life and your family life, that you take care of your family and your kids so that you don't have chaos at work and chaos at home.

I've watched too many people put so many hours into their jobs and then they have problems with their kids, or their marriages dissolve, and they destroy their ability to really function. Once that happens, you can't put it back together very easily.[3]

Once Larsen became chairman, he made a simple rule that he wouldn't travel on Sunday night for a Monday meeting. "Sunday night's our pizza night. I will get up at two o'clock in the morning on Monday morning, but if I have to leave the house at five o'clock on a Sunday, it ruins the whole family day. And my kids still talk about Sunday nights being pizza night, and it's the one thing in the craziness of my life—that we had a good time on Sunday night."

There is, of course, a great humanity and wisdom in what Larsen was saying. Greatness doesn't come from robots. Greatness comes from people who have figured out how to build around themselves a system that allows them to be almost an archetypal parental figure at work, the kind of person who helps others pursue their ultimate abilities in life.

Leading Others to Satisfy Their Innate Thirst for Triumph

It turns out that when properly channeled, this struggle for gratification invigorates the vast majority of people. Leaders who can make the constantly evolving, increasingly demanding competitive market tangible for employees can tap into the lifelong thirst for learning and betterment—a thirst innately present in every human.

So how to do it? Understanding the process of realizing potential requires insight into critical elements of human psychology, and indeed, all great leaders must be great psychologists. They have an acute understanding of human beings and what drives them. There are three keys to developing that innate thirst for triumph in others: making the real world palpable, encouraging a belief in the underlying purpose of the enterprise, and creating a sense of ownership over achievements.

Making the Real World Palpable

The first key in realizing your people's potential is to bring to the forefront the threats and uncertainties from the external environment and to make them palpable to your people. A. G. Lafley, chairman and CEO of Procter & Gamble, exemplifies this approach. "I want my people to feel the hot breath of the consumer," he said of his efforts to keep his company successful.[4] As with a champion sports team, success gets harder and harder to repeat, but by exposing his workforce to competition in palpable ways, rather than allowing it to relax into past performance success, Lafley is able to teach his people the gratification that comes with overcoming real-world challenges.

"Most people who work inside a company—the bigger the company the more this is true—are in a cocoon," Lafley told me. "And I want to bring the reality of the chaotic, competitive, survival-of-the-fittest world outside in. I like to be very explicit about whether we're winning or not winning at the first moment of truth—which is whether or not customers choose our product over the competitive product at the point of sale—which is very measurable. And then to look at how do we do in the second moment of truth—which is delighting our customers when they actually use our products, so that they keep coming back to use them."

Lafley uses both of these measurable indicators to make external market forces and P&G's performance within them very real for his people: "At the management meeting every year, I pull up a competitor, sometimes two, who is doing very well. And in front of the whole leadership team, I say, 'Here's a competitor that's, frankly, beating us right now. Here's how they're beating us. What are we going to do about it?' And these businesses have to come back to me with a strategy, a plan that will enable us to be winning the next time we get together."

Only the most masterful leaders can make tangible the competitive external environment in a way that allows their people to see how their personal efforts are translating into actual triumphs or losses in the outside world. As Lafley described, manifesting the maximum potential of a workforce requires consistent feedback about how people are doing compared with their competitors, and then providing people the tools and freedom to distinguish themselves with their performance.

This key tool of making the real world palpable for people will be discussed further in chapter 3. Yet this tool can't take hold if people don't believe that what they are doing *matters*.

The Role of Purpose in Realizing Potential

Lafley knows that the race he runs at P&G isn't a sprint; it's a marathon. And it is values and meaning that create that long-term success. "If you're a sprinter or you have a sprinter's makeup, it's not going to work; not in our industry and not in our business," he said. "It's . . . long-term sustainability, consistency. We are very purpose- and values-driven. We take the touching of lives, improving lives, seriously. We believe that our brands and product lines are designed, created, produced to make your life a little bit better every day. While it may sound cliché, I'm really here to help our people make a difference in the world by being the best that they can be."

While some simply cannot bear the idea of being number two, most human beings aren't so pathologically competitive that they can

drive themselves day after day just for the sensation of beating someone else, and neither are monetary rewards enough. In order to strive
to be extraordinary over a long period, therefore, most people must
feel they are working toward something meaningful, something that
deeply matters to them. Leaders need to make that meaning clear to
their people—and themselves. Being subservient to a higher purpose—as we'll learn later in the book—is a key attribute of great leadership.

To Herb Kelleher, a sense of purpose lay at the heart of his found-
ing Southwest Airlines during a time when the large, established carriers were doing everything possible to keep him on the ground. It
took him four years just to get permission to fly. When he finally got
his first airplane, he literally kissed it on the nose. What kept him
going through all those years of litigation with incumbent carriers?
His own outrage and idealism.

"I knew that if the country was going to behave like it was supposed to, it should welcome someone that proposed to provide a better quality of service at a far lower fare," he said. "There was
something wrong with our system if that didn't happen."[5]

Kelleher fought some of the lawsuits all the way to the Supreme
Court, and he litigated all the cases himself to avoid bankruptcy by
paying outside counsel. "What drove me through such dark times was
the conviction that I'm not going to let my vision be destroyed by allowing these other folks to manipulate and pervert the governmental
process. So it takes a lot of tenacity to get any company started. But in
some cases, it takes a sense of moral outrage. And I was morally out-
raged."

The fulfillment that we get from overcoming these obstacles—and
realizing our potential—can come from the pursuit of any number of
objectives, but what they all share is that they generate in an ongoing
way the opportunity for us to learn, grow, and better ourselves. Once

we experience the resultant gratification, we will naturally begin to seek it out ourselves. The pursuit of our betterment is so deeply gratifying that once we experience it, we will pursue it with intense focus. It is how we unleash the most lasting source of *passion* available to us.

When an organization has a leader who facilitates employees' opportunities to distinguish themselves in accomplishing meaningful tasks, that organization has an unbeatable competitive edge, because its employees can tap their innate thirst for triumph as natural motivation for their engagement. The highest-performing organizations invariably have a meaningful purpose for their existence, one that their people can easily embrace. And their leaders help their people readily see the difference the people make in furthering progress toward this purpose.

To be clear: when I talk about a company's purpose, I don't mean its mission statement. Obviously, these statements are noble in their intent and have an explicit, inspirational phrase that explains the organization's goals and purpose. But the mission statement is only a means to an end, and the end is this: increasing employees' engagement and making the company more successful *through* its employees' realization of their potential. When I say that great leaders must create a purpose or meaning for their employees, realizing the employees' potential can and should be that very purpose, and the mission statement is only a part of that puzzle.

For example, Jim Skinner, CEO of McDonald's, is famous for exhibiting a commitment to his people beyond his interest in the actual business of burgers. He entices employees to make their careers at the hamburger chain as a way of realizing their potential. Skinner should know how to do this—he was enticed by that same message early in his life. A non–college graduate who left a bad home environment to join the U.S. Navy, he nevertheless pursued self-improvement through role models, reading and educating himself. McDonald's was a place where he felt he could be successful: "I saw that people here respected each other and there was enough growth and opportunity in the company that I could become a key player, even though it could be in a small arena."[6]

"McDonalds is a place where you can grow based on your performance, not based on portfolio," he continued. "I know this because I didn't have a portfolio. That's something that continues to be a leadership tenant at McDonald's—our focus on people. I have a passion around allowing people who are underdogs, if you will, to be successful and be big players in big business because they've applied themselves and they are able to deliver results." Skinner makes a point, for example, to remind his people that of the eight CEOs who have run McDonald's, three started out in the restaurants, and one in the mailroom.

"To this day, I don't have a passion for hamburgers or cooking hamburgers," he said, "but I have a passion around pursuing continuous improvement in our business and focusing on people. People have the ability to take advantage of the opportunities here, and the sky is the limit."

The Role of Ownership in Realizing Potential

In order for people to experience the gratification that comes from distinguishing themselves, they must be able to own their achievements, to have a sense that these were a direct result of choices they themselves made. A sense of control over our own destinies is critical to how motivated we feel and our overall state of happiness. The most predictable aspect of people suffering from depression is that they have lost their sense of control, that they feel life's events are dictated to them rather than the other way around. Two people in the same circumstances will react to events in very different ways, according to how they interpret what is happening. The person who sees the future as malleable, who views the future more as a set of choices than as restrictions, will invariably be the happier and more energized of the two—and much more motivated to strive for his or her own goals.

In a deeper form, this sense of ownership over choices is critical to every leader; we will study it further as a sense of *agency* in the discussion of realistic optimism in chapter 3. But every human's ability to engage and rise to higher levels of achievement is based on this idea that people have some ownership of their successes and failures, and leaders need to understand this in order to bring that sense of triumph—and thus the thirst for triumph—to their people.

"You can give everybody instructions and then sit there impatiently pounding the table, wondering why it hasn't happened," said Marijn Dekkers, CEO of Bayer.[7] But, he said, "that tends to take more time than letting people figure out on their own, maybe with your help, so that they have ownership of what needs to be done and then execute better and faster." The key is to consciously hold back offering ready solutions.

"This is a new level of maturity that I don't think I had four, five, six years ago," Dekkers said. "I see this still with a lot of younger people who say, 'Okay, I know what needs to be done. I'm telling you what needs to be done; now go do it.' And then they wonder why it's taking so long."

Dekkers was talking about trying to manifest a system in which other people can be successful. This requires looking at the circumstance in which you are putting your people and making sure you are helping them to be successful in that circumstance. "As a leader with people working for you in a big organization," Dekker explained, "you have to realize people want a sense of control. You have to learn not to always tell them what to do, but let them figure it out themselves."

Yet as Dekkers pointed out, leaders, too, struggle with the desire for that same sense of control that their people need so badly. That is why learning to recognize and address your own competing impulses becomes critical for becoming the kind of leader you aspire to be. Moreover, this is why the idea of creating a context for your people to realize their potential is so important. Rather than doing it for them, you must clear the way for them to own their failures as well as their triumphs—or they will never know the urge for ever-higher levels of achievement.

We have covered the elements of realizing potential at a high level here. In the next few chapters, we will explore the common attributes of leaders who have demonstrated this process time and again in their own lives and created a context in which their people can experience it as well.

While we are all born with a longing to realize our full potential, we must first be taught to recognize this longing and then how to make it happen. The more you make these three catalysts a habitual part of your psychology, the more you can realize your potential, first as a guiding principle of your own behavior, and then as a guide for leading others.

2

Realistic Optimism

An Awareness of Actual Circumstances

Most people manage their anxiety under duress by using various coping mechanisms that mask the risks involved in the actual circumstances they are confronting. They ignore critical facts while relying on a belief that things will work out. Or they focus too closely on the wrong things—propping up a sapling when the whole forest is burning. But to be effective in today's economy, leaders must remain acutely aware of the reality of the challenges they face so they can focus their efforts on actions most likely to yield results. They must recognize that because today's economic world faces substantial ambiguity, they must strike a balance between the known and the unknown. In creating such a balance, leaders can maximize their odds of success—and engage a workforce—in the face of this uncertainty.

This attribute, which I will explain in detail in the next two chapters, is called *realistic optimism*. It's the first of the three catalysts that determine a relentless leader's capacity to realize his or her own potential, and the potential of others, in a world of ongoing duress.

To have realistic optimism, you as a leader must have an awareness of actual circumstances and a sense of agency. An *awareness of actual circumstances* means that you balance what is known and unknown to prepare for multiple plausible events. If you have a *sense of agency,* you believe deeply in your ability to alter your circumstances to suit your needs.

In this chapter, we take a closer look at awareness of actual circumstances and how it helps leaders maintain a sense of realistic optimism. An awareness of actual circumstances lends leaders a sense of humility, which is what primarily allows leaders to recognize their commonality with other human beings and to create organizations that continuously learn and improve. Through their sense of humility, leaders demonstrate the kind of elasticity critical for survival in today's business pressure-cooker. Moreover, these leaders model for their people the way to keep actual circumstances front and center by putting their own humanity on display; they have enough respect for their employees to be honest about their own shortcomings as leaders and to tell people the truth about the business. This creates a virtuous cycle that activates employee engagement around the very learning and improvement initiatives generated by the leader's keen grasp of the organization's struggles.

Humanity, in this sense, then, isn't about being soft or squishy. On the contrary, it's about being hard-nosed, realistic, and honest about the facts. Embodying the trait of humanity means that as a leader, you are challenging your people to acknowledge the cold, hard reality of the business together. If humility is about seeing the world for what it really is, humanity is about letting the world see you for what you really are. All the while, you're tapping into employees' innate drive for survival and thirst for realizing their own full potential to conquer the obstacles in their way, maximizing their own and the organization's effort and focus.

Do you have realistic optimism? This quick quiz, "Evaluating Your Level of Realistic Optimism," will give you a sense of where you fall.

Awareness of Actual Circumstances Versus Impervious Optimism

Why is an awareness of actual circumstances so hard—and what makes it so important—for leaders to see the world as it really is? Let's look as some examples of leaders who have addressed this question.

When we think of all the responsibility, setbacks, and other difficulties that a leader must face in today's work environment, the need for an underlying optimism is hardly surprising. But that optimism, something that is widely viewed as a valuable personality trait, can be an Achilles' heel for leaders. Optimism is a much more complicated concept than we often realize. Consider the following illustration involving a former employee of mine.

The first time I met "Steve" we were having lunch outside a hotel in Beverly Hills, and I remember he kept remarking about the beauty of our surroundings, the tremendous expanse of sky above us, and how terrific the food was. As we talked, that positive outlook was a continual presence. When we discussed the toll that constant travel could take, he spoke about how much he liked to travel and how he would always write ahead to friends in the area to find the best local-known restaurants. He truly believed there wasn't a problem that couldn't be figured out with the right attitude.

As research by prominent psychologist Martin Seligman has shown, that kind of optimism is critical to those in the insurance sales business and those who must handle rejection well; certainly it came in handy for Steve. Once I was at a meeting with him, when a senior HR executive was downright rude and acerbic to Steve. All Steve said

Evaluating Your Level of Realistic Optimism

You are hired to be CEO of a freight company, taking over for the retiring founder of the business. The outgoing leader was loved by both customers and employees and had always turned a profit, despite not raising rates for the past two years. Unfortunately, increases in fuel costs mandate that you raise your rates and cut some of your overhead, including staff, in order to maintain profitability. Please choose what most closely approximates your view of the following situations. This is a timed exercise: take no more than one minute to answer all four questions. Put a timer in front of you with the seconds ticking visibly away:

1. You are on the phone with an irate customer who has just learned of your rate increase. It appears you are likely to lose this customer's business. You view this situation as follows:

   a. You can't make every customer happy.

   b. There is always something you can do to improve a customer's experience.

2. The previous CEO was beloved by both employees and customers alike. If you were to guess, you would attribute his success as likely due to:

   a. Being fortunate enough to have been able to run the business during a more prosperous time.

   b. The result of hard work and persistent effort.

3. Impending staff cuts are inevitable, but you are concerned about how this will affect employee morale. You would approach the situation with the following view:

    a. The high level of anxiety created by staff cuts is unavoid-
able, and therefore we must be prepared to bear their reactions.

    b. There is much you can and should do during tough times to
keep employees hopeful. Therefore, you must take deliberate steps to bolster morale.

4. Loyalty and affection for the previous CEO are leading many
employees to question your decision making. You believe:

    a. I'm the CEO, and these people will inevitably come around
because I sign their paychecks. It'll just take some time.

    b. While their loyalty to their previous boss may be admirable,
I cannot allow it to express itself in a way that undermines
my authority.

These questions are designed to help you better understand your
level of realistic optimism and to show you the kind of situations in
which realistic optimism applies. The timed nature of the test is intended to re-create a decision-making situation under some duress.
For these four questions, the more times you answered "b," the
higher your level of realistic optimism, and therefore the higher
your overall level of realizing potential is likely to be.

Each question is designed to measure one of the two components that comprise realistic optimism. For instance, questions 1 and
3 determine whether you believe that outcomes are strongly determined by your own actions (the level of your sense of agency).
Questions 2 and 4 determine your level of awareness of actual
circumstances by whether you view complexity with unwarranted
certainty or practical realism. Are you stronger in one component or

the other? What do you still need to work on? By examining these insights, you can become more aware of mental habits that must change if you are to excel in realistic optimism—and ultimately to realize the potential in yourself and your people.

afterward was "I think that went really well. We're gonna close that sale!" His optimism allowed him to thrive in the sales profession, but it would render him completely ineffective in a leadership position.

Given the setbacks that every leader faces in today's environment of unprecedented competition, why wouldn't people with Steve's almost boundless optimism be able to use that as an asset? It is because that kind of optimism shows a disregard for a huge amount of critical information that is available in the world around him. Impervious optimism is a critical flaw because leaders have to process and address a tremendous amount of failure on their way to any success of significance. By examining their failures and why they happen, leaders determine what they must do differently to succeed. Furthermore, frustration and disappointment, though unpleasant emotions, are a critical internal thermometer that helps leaders measure the seriousness of a given setback. Great leaders are acutely aware when their efforts are encountering an obstacle, and they insist that their people be so as well.

Effective leadership requires an individual to take in both positive and negative messages, recognize their respective merits, and use the data to pursue a strategy that is most likely to yield positive outcomes in the future. Leaders need to remain painfully aware of the real uncertainties that exist and use them as part of their calculations to discover the best possible route to success.

And they must demand the same mentality of their people. To effectively realize potential in yourself and others, then, you must react to setbacks with the appropriate level of disappointment that reflects the seriousness of the problem so that your people also take the bad with the good. Impervious optimism blocks an awareness of actual circumstances and is a fatal flaw to anyone trying to lead in a world of ongoing duress.

What makes the negative feelings associated with setback even more essential is that, as we discussed in chapter 1, frustration, obstacles, and moments of doubt are actually *required* if we are to grow to our full potential. Beyond the practical implications of being realistic (i.e., knowing what problems need to be fixed), by facing those failures and deliberately pressing on in spite of them, a leader ultimately finds gratifying success.

Success by winning the lottery, on the contrary, does nothing to teach the gratifying process of realizing potential. People who do so get no closer to understanding their fundamental need for gratifying achievement. In fact, because wealth is often regarded as a public and visible signal of accomplishment, effortless attainment of wealth can actually push people further away from pursuing the kind of challenging work that leads to realizing potential, which can only be forged through adversity.

Similarly, a person born with extraordinary mental or athletic gifts often receives accolades throughout his or her early years without putting in as much effort as peers do for the same grades or athletic prowess. However, like free money, extreme talent can also be costly, because it can push people who possess it further from learning the lessons of how to realize potential. Ultimately, as their lives progress and they inevitably confront serious challenges or setbacks, they know nothing about the value of frustration, the discipline required to face their moments of doubt, and the gratification that comes from succeeding in spite of these challenges.

Gifts you receive are of far less perceived value because they cannot be internalized as something hard earned, something learned, or something that you otherwise had a personal role in obtaining. The journey to press on, to overcome adversity, must be derived because of a choice made. This is how self-esteem is built. This is how adults create an internal feeling that they matter—by choosing to play an essential role in bringing about something important but difficult to achieve. To be a master of realizing potential, you must be able to teach others how to overcome adversity.

This chapter examines how to develop an awareness of actual circumstances—especially when you look at yourself. As part of this examination, we'll look at the role humility plays in a leader's ability to face reality and how humility in turn helps craft the kinds of *elastic organizations* needed in today's pressured environment. We'll also learn how your ability to model pragmatism depends on the degree of humanity you exhibit, and how you can make the organization's drive for survival palpable for your people.

What Low Awareness of Actual Circumstances Looks Like

I interviewed "Tom" for a CEO position at a large insurance company we'll call Evergreen, Inc. Evergreen was in serious trouble because sales were dropping precipitously and lawsuits from customers threatened the company's solvency, creating a crisis of confidence both within its customer base and among its investors. The company desperately needed a leader that could restore the faith of its customers and investors.

Tom had served in another insurance company for over twenty years, but had left after being passed over for the CEO position. Evergreen's board was interested in bringing Tom in as its new CEO, but first wanted me to help the board members discover and understand why Tom had been passed over at his former company. Tom had begun his career in sales; his past was peppered with examples of turning underperforming units into best-in-class sales operations. Through our back-and-forth, the reasons for his sales success became clear—not only was he a tough, demanding manager, but he also had an uncommon level of professional drive.

"I started selling life insurance when I was in college and my father died," he told me. "I found out he had no life insurance, and when I asked my mother why, she told me no one had ever offered it to them. We were already a poor family, so I had to go to work if I was going to finish school." By the time he was twenty-two, he'd already achieved over one million dollars in sales. He attributed his success then and now to long, hard hours of work.

I asked Tom about his former boss, "Nick," reputed to be a tough leader. "I could deal with Nick," he said. "I'm a tough guy myself. I left home at sixteen. I have confidence because I built my success all on my own. Nick was a bully, but I grew up in a poor neighborhood and was used to bullies. If you stand up to a bully, they'll back off."

A difficult past can strengthen an individual as long as the person processes his or her own struggle as a part of these experiences and learns from it in observable ways. If people brush aside trauma from their past, however, and disassociate themselves from the experience, they will tend to avoid painful feedback rather than learn from it. This is a central mechanism that leads people away from an awareness of actual circumstances. Was that what was going on here?

I went on to ask Tom how his former boss Nick would describe him, and Tom replied, "Stubborn." He described how he and Nick had argued over how two employees' bonuses should be handled. "About six years ago," he began, "the regulators changed the rules around our accounting. If [our agents] sold other people's products rather than ours, we were ordered to give the same bonuses. One

year, the number one guy had placed a $600K sale for another in-
surer, with $1.5 million total. The second guy had sold $900K, all
[our company's products]. So Nick said he didn't want to give the
award to the guy that sold for the other insurer. I insisted that Nick
give it according to the rules. Nick called me ethically bullheaded. I
didn't care; what was right was right. I stood up to him. Nick got over
his anger, and we worked out giving an award to both of them."

While his anecdote describes an instance in which he stood up for
what he believed in, it is also important that in the story, Tom implic-
itly questions his former boss's ethics. In fact, throughout our conversation, Tom questioned in various ways the competence of virtually all
of his former colleagues. When I finally asked him why he decided to
leave his job after over twenty years at the company, he said he
couldn't support the CEO they selected. "He's not trustworthy," he responded. "He'll throw anybody under the bus to make himself look
better."

It struck me that Tom had almost nothing flattering to say about
any of the people he worked with, though records show that these
colleagues, some of whom had joined the company with or after Tom,
had been promoted ahead of him or over him. Either Tom was correct
and he was by far the most talented individual at his previous company but unfairly overlooked, or he was showing the classic sales-
person's impervious optimism *about himself* that characterizes so
many salespeople. Given the impressive long-term and ongoing
performance of his previous company, the latter was most plausible.

My hypothesis was verified during the case-study portion of our interview. Tom's critical-thinking skills benchmarked among the bottom third of senior executives. Furthermore, he generally refused to
listen to any constructive feedback regarding his performance.

Evergreen passed over Tom for the CEO role, and though he eventually did become CEO at another privately held insurance company,

at the time of publication of this book, eight months into his tenure, the company's bond rating had been lowered because of "an alarming exodus of senior leaders" under his command.[1] Because Tom's overconfidence in himself had isolated him from reality, he was unable to take others' criticism and address his own faults.

Overconfidence sets you up for failure because it isolates you from reality. In particular, you forget the creative role that doubt plays in getting your organization to improve. Doubt reveals the parts of reality that you missed. Once you lose your ability to doubt, you see only that which confirms your own competence.

Now contrast Tom's story with the story of Randy.

What Awareness of Actual Circumstances Looks Like

It was September 2008, and the collapse of AIG had just become public, rattling the world economy in an unprecedented way. AIG was considered by many the most stable company in the world, a reputation that earned it an investor rating higher than all of its competitors and a market position and reputation that was unmatched. Upon the company's collapse, it became frighteningly clear just how far out of touch with reality the insurance industry was as a whole—an industry whose very business model was supposedly built on its ability to accurately evaluate risk.

At this time, a team of colleagues and I went to meet the candidates for the CEO position at one of the world's largest insurance companies, an AIG competitor. The current CEO was planning for his replacement. Like AIG, this company was one of America's oldest and most trusted names in insurance, and at this time above all others, the successor would need an acute awareness of reality to do the job.

When we spoke to "Randy," one of a few front-runners for the position, he told us that AIG and others' credit default swaps were inexcusable and that the problems with these swaps were entirely predictable. Still, he said, his company had looked at swapping, too, but once he closely examined how it worked, he saw some serious exposure risks in the investments even as competitors were betting more and more heavily on them.

"Frankly, that perplexed me," Randy told me. "I ended up calling a friend at Goldman Sachs that was involved in the original creation of this market and asking him to explain to me what I was missing. He couldn't. After a few more of these conversations, I began to realize that given the extremely heavy bets these companies were making in these securities, they either didn't understand them, or they were violating their charter by investing in products that didn't fit their risk profile. I'm guessing that they just didn't understand them."

I asked Randy if that was why he ultimately stayed out of the credit default swaps business. His reply: "No—I never said that. Staying out entirely would have been stupid. The downside risk existed and had to be respected, but that just meant managing that risk." Randy therefore created a separate subsidiary unconnected to the rest of the corporation that did a small trade in these products, allowing him to participate in a very limited way without exposing the rest of the company. "Now when people look back, that move might seem like genius," he told me, "but at the time, it was simply about appropriately weighing risk and reward."

Throughout our conversation Randy showed himself acutely aware of actual circumstances. In his treatment of the credit default swaps issue, he showed that he had recognized both what was known and what remained unknown about the given set of circumstances, and he worked effectively with that ambiguity to derive an action plan that took advantage of differing possible outcomes. By insisting on seeing things for how they really were, even when short-term profitability and herd behavior had encouraged him to do otherwise, Randy showed himself to have a passion for confronting reality.

Because he refrained from putting an inappropriate level of certainty on situations, he kept his company's position flexible to address multiple possible scenarios. By acknowledging the nuances of what was known and unknown and articulating that he did not know which of these plausible scenarios would actually come to pass, Randy created an organization that possesses *elasticity*, a critical survival trait in today's competitive environment. Elasticity is thus a key benefit of acute awareness of actual circumstances. By insisting on this trait and modeling it for others, great leaders pass this trait on to their organizations.

But Randy's awareness of actual circumstances was directed inward as well. Let us now look at how this inward direction also benefited Randy and his people.

The Role of Humility in Facing Actual Circumstances—and Crafting Elastic Organizations

Once Randy discovered the risks unforeseen by his competitors regarding the credit default swaps, he found a way to take advantage of their upside. Acknowledging that his fears about their potentially catastrophic downside might never reveal themselves, he thus found a solution other than an all-or-nothing one. How did he show such foresight at a time when few others did? Randy's psychology kept him from putting an inappropriate level of certainty on situations, and he thus kept his company's position flexible to address multiple possible scenarios.

Specifically, Randy possessed the quality of humility (which I will define shortly), a mentality that allows a leader to acknowledge at least privately that he or she doesn't know how complex issues will turn out. Further, Randy acknowledged that success depended on rigorously reviewing different plausible outcomes and creating contingency plans to take advantage of these possibilities as circumstances eventually unfolded. This ability to walk freely around the gray, unknowable fog that exists within certain aspects of the future allows a leader to create an organization that can take advantage of multiple possible contingencies.

By acknowledging the nuances of what was known and unknown and articulating that he did not know which of these plausible scenarios would actually come to pass, Randy was showing himself as able to create an elastic organization. *Elasticity* is a key survival trait for companies in today's competitive environment, where the need to bend—but not break—is paramount.

Elasticity is a critical benefit of acute awareness of actual circumstances, and through that awareness—by insisting on and modeling it for others—masters of realizing potential pass on this trait to their organizations. As a result, organizations that maintain close touch with reality are better able to respond to events around them, elevating their level of elasticity within the ongoing turmoil that is today's global commerce.

Thus, the psychological elasticity—namely, the humility—that allows a leader to personally thrive in this environment creates an organization that can also thrive. Hallmarks of humility in a leader include several qualities: authenticity and the capacity for self-reflection, an absence of shame around personal failures and imperfections, and a heightened sensitivity and awareness of others.

Authenticity and the Capacity for Self-Reflection

As we walked through his career history, Randy's commentary was peppered with very frank assessments of his weaknesses, opinions on what he could have done better in each of his former roles, and comments on what he learned from each experience. "When I first started out [in insurance] seventeen years ago," he explained, "I wasn't sure what my role should be. I knew it couldn't be sales, since I stunk at remembering names." Later, he admitted a desire to improve his public speaking. And in a typical story, he explained how at one point, he had gotten too focused on lost earnings and missed some targets as a result; he then chose to supplement the company's income by selling some treasuries, which was a mistake. "Lost sight of the big picture there," he said, readily assessing his own performance.

Randy showed an uncommon capacity for confronting the full range of complexities regarding any given situation, even if doing so meant revealing his own personal weaknesses. He was authentic and humble about the unknowable and his own imperfections, and he showed a complete lack of shame in revealing them so freely. He possessed the acute awareness of actual circumstances—an awareness that this insurance company desperately needed in any CEO it selected. Indeed, this humility is a key part of a leader's self-awareness.

An Absence of Shame Around Personal Failures and Imperfection

When you as a leader possesses the kind of humility that enables your awareness of true circumstances, you can face all kinds of stimuli, from negative personal feedback to challenging market fluctuations to employees' or customers' emotional reactions, without experiencing internal disruption. This utter absence of shame around your miscalculations or outright failures is the critical differentiator of someone acutely in touch with actual circumstances and someone who is not. Randy clearly was.

"I made the decision at our group retreat last fall that each of our division leaders would present their accomplishments and goals for the upcoming year, rather than me doing it for them," Randy explained.

"At the time, I was trying to give everyone a sense of their shared responsibilities. But in retrospect, I should have been the only one who spoke—the group doesn't see me doing that enough. Frankly, I'm not that comfortable in front of large audiences. I still have to get better at that."

Heightened Sensitivity and Awareness of Others

Leaders who exhibit humility in particular have developed a heightened sensitivity to the feelings of others. Great leaders are very good at understanding the complex needs of their people and how to facilitate a context that can engage others' utmost effort. But in order to do this well, they themselves must be acutely sensitive. Sensitivity is an often misused and poorly understood concept. In business, it is generally talked about to describe a weak mind-set, one that responds to workplace conflict with neurotic agitation. The term *sensitive* is often a pejorative, suggesting that a person is neurotically worried about what other people think of him or her.

But it is well established that human beings with brilliant achievements tend to have significantly heightened sensitivities in all of their perceptions, including even their sense of taste or smell. High sensitivity refers to heightened radar, a more acute, broader spectrum of awareness of what is actually happening. When such an attribute is paired with an individual who is insecure about himself or herself, it can cause deep neuroses. But if a highly sensitive person also happens to be secure about his or her own strengths and imperfections, a heightened awareness of feedback from the environment becomes a critical asset.

Sensitivity, then, is a critical asset in leadership. Indeed, aspiring leaders must be sensitive if they wish to engage their workforce in a way that realizes their maximal potential. Great leaders are highly sensitive in that they are acutely aware of the reactions of their people, the rhythms of the workplace, and the subtle, often unsaid shifts in the attitudes of their customers. Heightened awareness is not selective—it exposes leaders to a wide spectrum of data that can include stinging feedback.

Of course, leaders already are the target of an extraordinary amount of criticism, some of it public. They can't simply turn off their minds to the noise, and because great leaders have a heightened awareness of what is happening around them, they are exposed to ongoing, potentially disruptive feedback. This is why, when talking about themselves, the leaders I interviewed seemed so comfortable in their own skin. Anyone meeting them gets an immediate experience of their realness and authenticity. But what you are actually experiencing is the leaders' unusual facility for openly relating to their environment without fear of threat to their own sense of well-being.

I observed this quality in Miles White, CEO of the life sciences company Abbott. I asked him how he manages the emotional swings anyone has to bear as a CEO. "You can say all you want that a CEO has to have thick skin," White said. "It's the last thing any good CEO has. If you're the right kind of servant leader, you have to have *thin* skin. If you're completely oblivious, the 'I've arrived, imperial monarch,' well, you probably don't have thin skin. You're so clueless that you're going to be dead meat before you know it. The best CEOs that I've seen are very sensitive. They're sensitive about their performance and about their people. All of my top people are high achievers, and they are all highly sensitive."[2]

What defines both the impervious optimist and the master of engaging a workforce to realize potential in a world of ongoing duress is their sensitivity to feedback and how they interpret it. Impervious optimists have a narrow sensitivity to the world around them. They can ingest only positive interpretations of events or risk imploding from negative feedback. Great leaders like Randy and White have developed enough comfort within themselves, their own traits and vulnerabilities, to absorb negative information without collapsing, and they consider the criticism a meaningful window into how they can better themselves or more effectively reach their goals.

Learning about yourself is always gratifying, no matter what stage of life you are in or what professional success you have had. CEOs are no different—they love learning because of the gratification it brings. Realizing potential creates a cycle of self-improvement, in which you develop an ever-increasing sense of your own capabilities and an increasing thirst to improve upon them. Your acute awareness of actual circumstances becomes a critical step in realizing your and others' potential.

Being acutely aware of both your strengths and your weaknesses is a delicate balance to achieve—and to model to your people. It's not enough just to be aware of what's going on around you; you also need to demonstrate this awareness for your people, so that they too are encouraged and inspired to have the same understanding of the world. How do great leaders achieve such a balance? By showing their humanity.

Modeling Awareness of Actual Circumstances by Humanizing Yourself

While leaders must maintain a sense of humility, or accurate self-awareness, to make the best decisions and to grow to their full potential, they must also project this very human image to their people. Good leaders must reject the paradigm of the aloof business executive who makes nearly perfect decisions alone in the C-suite. If you follow the old paradigm and ignore the inadequacies that exist, then your behavior suggests that it is OK for others to do the same. In this sense, humanizing yourself goes hand-in-hand with the humility it takes to see the world for what it really is. By then showing the ongoing hard work that it takes to be great—the effort required to overcome obstacles, frustration, and self-doubt—you show by example what is required to realize your potential and thrive in the face of intensifying competition. So while humility allows you to see things as they are, humanity allows the world to see you as you really are.

Today's masterful leaders humanize themselves in different ways, depending on their personal style and what is most natural for them. Some broadcast their life stories of challenges and obstacles overcome, such as David Novak's autobiography, *From Trailer Park to CEO*. Herb Kelleher has freely shared stories of his early life, in which he was raised by a single mom during wartime. A. G. Lafley publicly lists his own failures—he talks about why he failed, what he could have done better, and what he learned from the experience. Lafley's list includes his leadership failure in P&G's global beauty segment, which didn't make its numbers under his direction in the late 1990s; Lemon Dash detergent, which failed because it offered nothing different from existing products; and an Olay cosmetics line that he had to discontinue after poor consumer testing. Kevin Sharer, CEO of Amgen, has his direct reports list his strengths and weaknesses annually for the company's board, and he even has a painting of General Custer in his office because earlier in the CEO's career, Sharer was occasionally guilty of thinking too much of himself—just as Custer had been before he experienced his famous last stand.

Repeatedly as I sat with the CEOs who were considered masters of their domains, I had the same visceral reaction: *they are so comfortable in their own skin.* They don't seem threatened or anxious when talking about their mistakes. They can talk about their faults or errors without agitation, and never describe themselves in a way that sounds heroic—just the opposite. Whatever accomplishments they have made in their history, these CEOs insist that it was the result of intensely hard work, sacrifice, and moments of doubt before the ultimate experience of triumph, and that there were plenty of occasions of failure along the way. But as living examples of publicly admired individuals who face and must overcome setbacks, they are able to credibly model for their people the deliberate, intense focus and collective effort needed to bring about positive outcomes. In this way, these leaders teach realistic optimism by example. These expressions of humanity from today's most successful CEOs mirror a demand that their people face their own mistakes and fallibility as well.

As mentioned earlier, the psychological makeup that allows these leaders to talk about their failures with such openness is their humility, notably a lack of shame regarding their fallibilities. They can face their failures without threat of personal collapse. It is what allows them to be acutely aware of, and deal with, actual circumstances. But as a leader, it will be your *humanity* that your people see and will want to emulate, so that they too can realize their full potential.

Failures do elicit a feeling of deep frustration in masters of today's competitive climate, but these downfalls do not elicit shame. Shame reflects a much deeper uncertainty about your own competence and is much more threatening to your sense of stability. If you feel recurring shame around your failures, you ignore their existence altogether. This defense mechanism is useful in protecting your short-term sense of self-esteem, but in the long run, it does the exact opposite. You no longer have the opportunity to face a challenge and ultimately conquer it, which is the surest way to realize your potential. To become a great leader, you must not shy away from those moments about which you feel ashamed.

Because shame is one of the most difficult human emotions for people to bear, either within themselves or even to witness others experience it (empirical research studies strongly correlate feelings of shame with increased avoidant behaviors), leaders must balance their reactions to shame. Shame sharply pierces our sense of identities. To stay in touch with our failures is to tolerate our experience of shame associated with it. It is a critically important balance for leaders to be able to maintain and to model for their people.

Before he was CEO of Amgen, Sharer was the former president of General Electric and a former executive vice president at MCI. He illustrates how a leader in today's economy stays acutely aware of obstacles and is honest about failure, rather than allow it to devolve into shame, without being overwhelmed. "You have to operate in a bit of an out of body way," he told me. "It's not okay to get angry. It's not okay to cut people off and be impatient. You try very hard to create an environment where people feel tension to perform but also know that they're going to be treated with complete respect as human beings. That's the only way you're going to get the best out of them."[3]

Sometimes it helps to think about the job metaphorically, he added. He imagines himself as the driver on an 1840 wagon train heading west, not knowing exactly what tomorrow will bring.

> You've got to find a way through this unknown place to your destination. You've got to be able to understand the feelings, hopes, aspirations, worries of everyone on the wagon train. You've got to minister to those, in a way. You've got to have a vision for the future that gives your people the confidence that it actually can be achieved.
>
> You know, it's exhilarating some days. Some days, boy, the natives are not very friendly. Some days, we're fording in the stream. Some days, we're crossing a beautiful meadow. This metaphor helps me keep perspective.

While the wagon train analogy helps Sharer manage the frustrations of leading in an extremely challenging environment, he has also aggressively put systems in place to receive feedback on his actions that *aren't* working. "If you're not getting better as a CEO, you're getting worse," Sharer said. "Nobody stays the same. Some people who get this job think that they just got into the NFL Hall of Fame. When the reality is, it's just like a rookie starting quarterback. And guess what? About half of them don't do too well."

The portrait of General Custer on Sharer's office wall serves as a daily reminder of what he still needs to learn. "I got that picture when I first got the job here," he said. "I knew in my own makeup that confidence can be a strength or weakness. The weakness of confidence is arrogance and overconfidence. And so I thought it wouldn't be a bad idea to have a guy on my wall who underestimated the enemy, overestimated his own ability, and lost it all. That's just a good little cautionary tale."

So the challenge then becomes, how do you learn and grow? How do leaders find ways to receive constructive, honest, appropriate feedback regularly, in a world where few people in any stage of their career enjoy such a luxury? Sharer holds an annual meeting for the express purpose of counteracting "CEO syndrome" and forcing his team to be straight with him about what he does well, but, most importantly, what he needs to do better.

"The team knows I care and will listen," he said. "They know that what they say matters, so they take it seriously. I tell them, 'Look, I know I'm a good athlete. I'm not Michael Jordan, but I'm a shooter that's pretty good. I know I can play this game. What I want to know is, what shots do I really need to work on? Let's talk about those.'" The formal feedback system is one of many ways in which Sharer approaches his work as a student, a life-long learner who is willing to show his human side. But Sharer's behaviors go beyond traditional feedback analytics.

When he discusses himself and his history, he shows himself as vulnerable and sincere about how much he has had to change.

> You know, the reality behind the résumé is that there were a few times where it was a close run, and it could have gone the other way. Not because I behaved badly or anything else. It's just, hey, that's how life is. And so I came to appreciate the need for feedback and to continually get better. When I left GE at forty-one years old, I was probably at my zenith of arrogance. And the experience at MCI was very difficult. It served a much larger and really beneficial purpose in my own development, because when I left MCI for my job here, I was a lot smarter guy than when I had left GE three years before. And if I hadn't had the MCI experience, I could have blown up here.

Sharer's insistence throughout our conversation that his success was far from preordained reveals his acute awareness of actual circumstances. His openness to the very real possibilities that events could have unfolded unfavorably throughout his life is an essential part of his insistence of a clear-eyed view of his life choices. This kind of realism is at the heart of the adaptive capacity leaders need to have: to authentically believe in the value of self-improvement, leaders must also authentically embrace how their past imperfections had very real, and sometimes costly, consequences.

For example, Sharer described how two of his best people almost blew up over tension with each other, and how he was able to claim his own role in the issue. "I had assigned my two key guys to resolve a problem," he told me. "I just said, 'Would you guys please figure this out?' They didn't have a shared reality, and it wasn't clear who was supposed to do what. Soon their differences of opinion were starting to cascade down. It was really tearing the company apart."

Once it finally dawned on him that he might have had a role in the conflict from the beginning, he asked himself honestly what part of it he owned, and then he set things right. "I came up with a list about that long"—he spread his arms wide—"of my part of the problem. And when I briefed them the next Monday. I said, 'Look, guys, before I tell you what's gone wrong and what we need to do, let me tell you what I haven't done.' That cleared the air, and then we found a way to fix things. In fact, we got stronger as a team because of going through this fire together."

Thus Sharer made it nearly impossible for his two subordinates to continue their loop of dysfunction. And this approach points to an important tension that great leaders must balance: knowing when to intervene in a problem to set things straight—and when to create a context in which the participants can take responsibility. In either case, managing today's sophisticated workforce entails modeling for subordinates the very behavior they need to adopt themselves. That means leaders need to genuinely acknowledge their personal role in any problem. "If you're a CEO saying, 'I've got a great strategy but my team just can't implement it'—that's not owning the problem," Sharer said.

Great leaders often find that sharing with their subordinates the load of responsibility is essential for gaining the full engagement of a sophisticated workforce. Visibly holding yourself to the same level of accountability that you hold your people to can be powerfully motivating to knowledge workers—it forces them to do the same. And by doing so, they begin to experience the gratification that comes from realizing their potential. What's more, they feel a sense of community, because their colleagues are equally committed to doing the same.

Even so, Sharer's openness about his own fallibility is very different from the attitudes of the generation of CEOs who preceded him, many of whom he worked for. Honest and open self-reflection is something that has emerged only recently, among today's most admired leaders. "Some of it's generational," Sharer explained. "Some of it is an adaptive requirement. With all the things that are going on in today's workplace, if you're not a little bit self-reflective and self-aware, you're not going to make it. I think some of it is the fact that in America, authority is less and less revered, and this is not a bad thing. The people who work here are plenty smart, and they demand to be treated with respect. You won't be accepted as a leader unless you are willing to really engage."

The competitive environment has changed so fundamentally, in fact, that CEOs need self-reflection much more now than ever before. The pace of change in the world today requires it. For Sharer, it comes down to this: "If a CEO is not reflective and welcoming and respect-ful, he or she won't get the best team, and no CEO alone can navigate successfully for long through the complexity that we face. If you think that you've got all the answers and you're just going to shout rudder or-ders all day long, then the ship's going to go aground eventually."

The good news is that these behaviors can be learned. "I do believe that leaders can develop," Sharer said. "I think it's more learned than it is born. There's something about charisma that you can't teach, but that's not all that important. People in the right environment with the right motivation and the right coaching, they can develop enormously. More than anyone thought."

Throughout our conversation, Sharer revealed how a strong leader continuously pursues self-improvement and models an appropriate level of humility. This dose of realism is important: because he has allowed himself to be aware of the actual circumstances around him, Sharer is able to think of himself as a life-long student, continuously learning and evolving to better adapt to the challenges at hand. In today's global economy, a leader cannot pursue learning and self-improvement intermittently. Only those who see themselves as contin-uously learning and improving to better meet the emerging challenges around them can rise to the top. Further, leaders who cannot tolerate this level of self-reflection and intentional effort to improve will lose, because not only do they fall behind their competitors, but they also fail to model for their people the kind of continuously adaptive effort required to succeed in a fluid environment.

Next, let's look at how leaders can help their people develop an acute awareness of the actual circumstances the organization is facing.

Making the Organization's Drive for Survival Palpable

As we learned in chapter 1, making the real world palpable is an important way to lead others to realize their potential. Making more tangible the very real competitive threats from the outside world is an important part of a leader's awareness of actual circumstances, because it helps remove the cocoon of routine daily life that shields employees from the tumult of the marketplace. The more explicit you make those threats, the more effectively you tap your employees' acute drive to survive. In making your people keenly aware of the ever-encroaching competitive field, you give them collective opportunity to distinguish themselves through triumph. Combining the will to survive with the gratification of triumph is a powerful force.

In an intensely competitive environment, an organization's weaknesses will inevitably make it vulnerable to decay. The discipline to face our own inadequacies requires conscious effort, and most organizations unconsciously foster avoidance of such topics. But realizing your potential requires that you tolerate the discomfort of honestly confronting and addressing your inadequacies.

Jim Kilts did just this at two companies: at The Gillette Company, during his historic turnaround of the floundering American business icon after he became CEO in 2001, and at Nabisco in 1998. In both cases, he laid out for his team members clear metrics benchmarks regarding their performance, forcing them to face the cold facts of their mediocrity, take ownership of inadequacies, and stoke their internal hunger to do better. He went after the avoidance habits at Gillette with a vengeance. As will be detailed in chapter 3, he made the sales team report its numbers on a daily basis—a continuous, insistent drumbeat that served to drive reality home: change or perish.

"When I came into Gillette, even though sales were flat and earnings were flat for five years, they thought they just ran into a little bit of bad luck," Kilts told me. Gillette had long been a successful eastern company, based in Boston, with a company culture that took pride in its history of being one of the all-time great U.S. companies. When it fell onto hard times, people in the company were pointing the finger at everyone but themselves.

At Gillette, once Kilts made the problems and the objective clear, he let everyone know that he'd be measuring the solutions. Only by facing an honest appraisal of how you underperform can you experience the sharp pain that comes from not living up to expectations. But by helping people earn the pride and fulfillment that comes from improvement and building something that excels, you can help them earn the sense that they are playing a critical role in something extraordinary.

At the end of the next chapter, you'll find some suggestions and exercises for improving your ability to stay aware of actual circumstances. But first, let's move now to the second essential component of the catalyst of realistic optimism: a sense of agency.

3

Realistic Optimism

A Sense of Agency

Every time that I'm called in to work with a CEO who is in trouble, I'm asked, Is the executive savable? Is it worth trying? And while the answer is rarely simple, *the single most telling factor is the individual's sense of agency.* Change *is* possible; everyone is teachable and can grow and improve. But if the person has a low sense of agency, then change will be extraordinarily tough, costly, and lengthy and will require highly skilled intervention.

Sense of agency, the second component of realistic optimism, refers to the degree to which people attribute their circumstances and the outcomes they experience to being within their own control. People tend to be inward or outward in their explanation for life events. For those who choose external explanations for what is happening—I didn't get promoted because my boss is stupid, I only got this job because my dad called someone—long-term success becomes much more difficult.

No phrase better codifies a low sense of agency than the all-too-common "If it is meant to be, it will be." Incredibly circular in its logic, within this phrase is perceived freedom from any culpability in the events of our lives. For adults who cannot tolerate the anxiety brought on by knowing that they are largely responsible for what happens to them, this mantra can bring a temporary sense of deluded relief. But there is no genuine escape from the reality that our path to gratification or regret is largely up to us. No amount of disowning will change this, regardless of how many times we tell ourselves otherwise.

For those who look inwardly for explanations, learning and behavior change become much more plausible. Human beings vary wildly on the degree of influence they believe their actions will have on outcomes. The perspective of your own agency in the world is highly subjective, and realizing potential in a stressful climate requires seeing and explaining events in a way that suggests that outcomes are largely contingent on your own behaviors. It is one of the essential factors that enable you to manifest relentless leadership in trying times, both for yourself and for others.

In this chapter, we'll look at why a sense of agency can be such a game changer for aspiring leaders. We'll learn how to energize a workforce by intensifying its sense of agency and how to use metrics and feedback to help your people face reality. We'll also explore how to recognize both a high and a low sense of agency in others. The chapter concludes with some advice and exercises to help increase your level of realistic optimism in general.

High Sense of Agency Changes the Rules

Because exceptional leaders believe that their own actions will largely determine outcomes, these leaders, even in the most challenging circumstances, tend to do things that can appear unconventional to others. Throughout their actions, *their sense of agency expands the freedom they feel within their situation.* As a result, great leaders often

use seemingly unconventional ways to approach challenges. They ignore limitations that would inhibit anyone else, because of their high
sense of agency. Their self-determination generates a sense of opportunities where others see none.

This is in part why such leaders appear courageous to others—
great leaders do not perceive the same boundaries that others do.
Their sense of agency infuses creativity into their approach, one that
often unties knots that others see as unmanageable.

One of the most creative managerial minds I've ever encountered,
Chevron's CEO Dave O'Reilly, illustrates this point. When he was
only thirty-two years old, he took over the management of a Califor-
nia chemicals plant. Three other people with more experience in the
organization had rejected the position because the situation was so
messy. O'Reilly had only a background in refining and petroleum
products, so he was intrigued by the specialty chemicals business.

His story of his first day on the job—during a month-old strike—
illustrates how his sense of agency allowed him to approach the problem in a creative and fluid way. His career in the oil industry since
that time has shown him the importance of teaching his people to
approach their jobs with that same sense of agency. His tenure began
with a key move on his part: arriving that first morning at the picket
line and getting out of his car.

"It was a damp morning, and there were about twenty people hud-
dling around the gate with picket signs," he told me. "I just wanted to
say hello and see if I could establish some understanding of how they
were feeling. So I got out, introduced myself, talked to them a little bit,
and found out that, unlike what you might expect, they weren't negatively aggressive. They had been out for a month by this time, and obviously, they were concerned about how long this was going to go on."[1]

That simple yet unexpected act at the picket line helped to break
the ice and open up communications quickly around the workers'
concerns regarding the plants' safety and reliability. "I think we got a

much faster running start as a result of that early interaction," O'Reilly said. "The word got out pretty quickly that I had gotten out of the car and talked to them. It was a very simple motivation at the beginning, but it turned out to have a much bigger impact than [on] just the handful of people I talked to at the gate. It certainly helped create a better work environment later." Because O'Reilly had believed that he could make a difference, he took the opportunity to do something that others would have deemed pointless.

Not too many newly appointed managers would have approached such a seemingly adversarial group on their first day of work, particularly in such an informal way. But O'Reilly's psychology was not focused on his positional authority or the conventional expectations that this would bring, such as initiating his first contact with unhappy workers through a more formal meeting with their labor leaders. He simply saw a group of colleagues outside early on a cold morning, people that he was about to begin working with, and wanted to meet them and better understand the factors that motivated their protest. People with a high sense of agency don't tend to focus on conventional ways of doing things. Instead, they approach each situation in a way that weighs the needs of the individual moment versus what others might consider the appropriate norms for handling it.

O'Reilly's discarding of conventional approaches to complex issues has enabled Chevron to improve upon an often adversarial relationship with the community it serves and encourage a more constructive, partnership approach. This requires a focus on mutual interests rather than on areas of disagreement. In doing so, O'Reilly is exposing his belief that Chevron bears responsibility for bettering its relationship with people who are outside the oil industry and who hold a very negative view of its business. His focus on establishing mutual understanding represents a shift from the way big oil executives historically have engaged with the public. It's made O'Reilly a spokesperson for his industry, for example, participating in televised debates with Sierra Club leaders about the future of energy.

> I was raised in a small country [Ireland], and when you're raised in a small place you have to learn to look through the lens of things from other people's perspectives. The things that I graphically remember growing up are the Cold War years and the Cuban missile crisis. I was in high school at the time, sitting there in a country of three million people, and these behemoths are ready to blow the world apart at each side of you. You're saying to yourself, there's nothing you can control about this other than trying to put yourself in the shoes of the people that are the instigators of this big clash. We were witness to the dramatic consequences wrought by two adversaries' interpretations of each other's intentions.

O'Reilly, on the other hand, believes that there *is* something we can control about most situations. His sense of agency allows him to see how bridging the gap between two seemingly blood enemies is possible—if some mutual understanding and respect of each other's perspective can be reached. Complex, potentially adversarial relationships, whether they're between countries or between environmentalists and oil companies, are among the most common and difficult knots to untie. But in today's global workplace, people must recognize how—and *that*—their own approach to the problem can either exacerbate these obstacles or bridge the space between two parties.

Dave O'Reilly's actions show how critical a high sense of agency is to managing a highly diverse, global workforce and customer base. He also insists that his people learn how to do the same. To that end, he tells employees that they have a part in shaping the way that big oil is seen by the public, that their actions help determine that view, and that to some degree it's up to them to repair any bad reputation the company might develop. It's not someone else's fault, someone else's problem: their actions have an impact. He gave an example: "The important thing is when we experience bad press, we have a responsibility to ensure that we're doing a good job in communicating. When people don't understand us, it isn't necessarily their fault. We might not be communicating well enough."

By emphasizing his employees' own responsibilities and their agency, he has created at Chevron a firm with high recruitment acceptances (70–80 percent) and increased executive retention rates. People who feel that their jobs make a difference tend to want to stay put: O'Reilly's employees consistently score high in the top quarter percentile for employee engagement when Chevron is benchmarked against other oil companies. By insisting that his people recognize their own responsibility for facilitating this cooperative action, he shows them how Chevron must take ownership for not just serving the world's energy needs, but also actively addressing various communities' concerns about how best to do so.

Today's masterful leaders stress how success is dependent on our own actions and that regardless of outside events that may be beyond our control, it is how we interpret and react to them that will determine our success. This is what makes a sense of agency such a critical component of identifying creative opportunities to solve seemingly intractable issues.

Energizing a Workforce by Intensifying Its Sense of Agency

One of the most critical ways relentless leaders increase the sense of agency of their people, especially in a stressful environment, is to increase the observable level of control the people have over their jobs. This is how Irene Rosenfeld, CEO of Kraft Foods Inc., went about transforming an organization that was suffering from a demoralizing period of underperformance. Rosenfeld cited overcentralization as one of the key problems that needed to change. I asked her how that phenomenon affects employees' ability to work at their full potential.

"You have to put yourself in the shoes of someone who feels that decisions are outside their control," she said. "They have no authority. It's what you might expect from people living under a communist regime. Over time, their sense of hopelessness and despair eventually leads them to just throw up their hands and let events overtake them. And I saw that feeling around the company when I first got there. That had to change."

But in an organization that previously had too little accountability and responsibility, infusing a workforce with these qualities can be a tricky business. Great leaders find ways to flip the switch of engagement, even in people who hadn't been hired for that ability.

"I've joked about the fact that we've given everybody the car keys, but not everybody knows how to drive," Rosenfeld said. "It is about capability building, and we have been focused on helping our managers become general managers and teaching them what they need to know from a broader business perspective. Most will make it, but a few will not."

Rosenfeld agrees that the fundamental desire for autonomy and the freedom to realize one's potential on the job is universal—certainly it crosses the global borders among which Kraft operates. Yet she sees the starting point for that freedom as quite different from market to market and culture to culture: "I would suggest that probably the United States is the freest of all of our cultures and therefore most likely to be seeking empowerment [compared with] some other cultures. So there are some cultural differences in terms of how [the various global markets] respond to the directions that I'm setting. But I think they're all operating within their own history as well as operating in the spirit with which we're trying to move."

Giving people an increased sense of agency is a powerful trigger for increasing their sense of responsibility over their own actions. For the vast majority of people, this invigorates their level of engagement with their jobs.

The dramatic increase of people's motivation toward their work was first explored in a landmark paper by Harvard psychologist Robert White. In a 1959 paper titled "Motivation Reconsidered: The Concept of Competence," White first proposed the concept that people are most strongly motivated by opportunities to experience an expanded sense of their own effectiveness.[2] Since then, motivational theory has repeatedly shown that people are motivated by a feeling of efficacy and competence and that workplaces that acknowledge this by giving people a sense of control over their own jobs are more successful in motivating people to work harder.[3]

To experience the gratification that comes from distinguishing yourself, you must be able to feel ownership of your achievements—that these were a direct result of choices you made. Especially in an environment of ongoing duress such as what we face today, where things around us can quickly begin to feel beyond anyone's power to alter, giving people a sense of control over their own destiny helps determine their level of motivation and overall state of happiness. Two people in the same circumstances will react to events in very different ways, depending on how they interpret what is happening. The person who sees upcoming situations as up to himself or herself and who is more aware of the choices available in these circumstances rather than the restrictions will invariably be the happier and more energized of the two—and much more motivated to strive for his or her goals.

Using Metrics and Feedback to Help Your People Face Reality

It is your ultimate responsibility as a leader to teach your people to face reality. That means helping demonstrate that what we do on a daily basis is very much under our control, and that our boundaries of operation are probably much wider than we think. To enable your workforce to realize its potential, you must be very clear about the actions that will lead to positive results. Recursive, accurate feedback mechanisms, such as specific metrics and benchmarks, can show individuals how they are doing, both their moments of success and where they stumble. It is critical that you allow individuals to recognize for themselves the particular habits that help or hinder them. If the consequences of their actions are made clear and immediate, most people can correct their problem behaviors.[4] You can reinforce the individual's sense of agency even more if you concentrate on giving feedback strictly in terms of outcomes of the individual's efforts and leaving it up to the individual to then decide how to change those efforts.

Gordon Bethune, former CEO of Continental Airlines, offers a powerful example of this kind of reinforcement and the effect it can have on helping people to realize their potential under duress. When Bethune was only twenty-two, he received his first leadership position, managing a navy aircraft maintenance team, most of whose members were much older than he was. But within twelve months, navy operations classified his team as the best in the nation. I asked him the secret to his effectiveness and how he instilled that same sense of accomplishment in his direct reports.

He told me that his first job had been as a mechanic, and he knew the difference between how fast he got something done when he really cared about doing them—and when he didn't care. He approached his unit knowing he had to find a way to get the group to want to fix airplanes as quickly as possible. "As their leader, you've got to respect your people, to talk with them in their language," he said. "I shared all the information I had with them—everything about our performance metrics—about how we'd done with our tasks that day, where we stood in terms of our performance with other units. You tell people how to keep score, and reward them for it. But you have to make sure you're using the right scorecard."

Bethune used the same philosophy as CEO of Continental Airlines. "It couldn't be about high-minded notions—it had to be practical, straightforward, [logical], and measurable," he said. "Simplicity of mission is key, so for us it was, what is it that people really want from an airline? Clean, safe, reliable [air transportation]. That's the core of how any customer would grade us, so that's how we had to grade ourselves. And every one of our employees knew how we were doing on each of these, and they'd get rewarded for their success."

When Bethune started at Continental, the airline was ranked last in on-time flights. He promised every employee a $65 bonus each month that Continental was in the top half of airlines in on-time performance. The first month, Continental shot up the list. "How much structural change do you think they got done in those first weeks?" Bethune said. "Getting our planes moving faster was purely about collaborative effort." Keeping that record going meant adhering to the same basic principles. "Keep what constitutes success simple and believable for your employees. It has to make practical sense to them if it's going to work. Then measure and reward it," Bethune said. Continental's on-time flight record went from the worst to the best, and then it stayed consistently at the top of on-time rankings. Bethune periodically raised the target even higher, again promising to reward employees. If they upped Continental's overall percentage of flights that were on time over the previous quarter, then the company would distribute a special $65 bonus check monthly to each employee. Its numbers improved every quarter.

"They enjoyed the challenge of it," Bethune said. "It made their jobs fun, and because they were having fun, they made sure our customers were having fun. And we made sure they felt recognized for it. Anytime one of our managers got a reward, they were expected to accept the reward only on behalf of the team . . . The recognition was more about the hard work of others, not about them."

Bethune's practices of providing ongoing, clear performance metrics for his people engaged their natural desire to experience triumph. By clearly connecting the effect of employees' personal workplace behaviors with the actual performance of the airline, he helped them take ownership of the enterprise's success and experience the gratification that resulted.

The degree to which employees realize their potential is found in their day-to-day, minute-to-minute decisions, almost none of which are witnessed by their superior. There are an infinite number of opportunities for people to make a choice, for example, whether to focus their moments on their most immediate work priority or turn to any number of potential distractions. Manifesting maximum potential requires creating a context in which every employee understands the most valuable specific activities he or she could address in that moment and how to do so most efficiently so that the employee could move on to the next task. But even more importantly, it means finding ways to benchmark their performance against compelling targets and rewarding their achievement.

A sense of agency is so critical to leadership, because high-performance organizations find ways to help their people do their work well every day. While it is remarkably common for great successes or failures to be explained as the consequence of a single dramatic moment, any notable achievement is indisputably the product of a countless series of choices that trace well back into time. The seemingly mundane nature of the daily routine required to reach profound goals is surprising to most people, and it rarely makes for a compelling headline in a magazine article. But the answer to great accomplishment in a world of unprecedented distractions lies in the deliberate, focused discipline that manifests itself in everyday choices. Without a culture that emphasizes a high sense of agency, an organization cannot evoke this discipline.

What a High Sense of Agency Looks Like

A high sense of agency permeates the mind-set of great leaders, in how they view both their own actions and those of their people. An excellent example of this is Chris Van Gorder, CEO of Scripps Health System. Van Gorder began his career just after college as a police officer. In 1978, Van Gorder was injured on the job while responding to a domestic disturbance call. He spent the next year in orthopedic hospitals and rehabilitation centers, learning to walk again, but his physical condition forced him to retire as a police officer.

Van Gorder experienced a setback in his life that would have staggered anyone. But instead of blaming his accident and spending the rest of his life inactive, Van Gorder took initiative and adapted to the circumstances, reestablishing control over his life. "I figured I could no longer be a cop, but I knew something about hospital systems at this point," he told me. "I'd been on the patient side of things long enough."[5] He applied for a position at Orthopedic Hospital in Los Angeles as its head of security and got the job. Instead of just acting like a victim of bad luck, Van Gorder found himself resurrecting his professional prospects and reinforced his confidence in himself:

regardless of external factors, he could find a way to work within their constraints to achieve success.

Van Gorder later applied this mind-set in helping his people turn around the horribly dysfunctional hospital system he stepped into at Scripps. Relations between management and employees were terrible, the hospital was losing money, and the previous CEO had just been fired for the organization's poor performance. The most urgent problem Van Gorder decided to address? Accountability. And, he told me, it's an imminently teachable quality to instill in your people.

"I met with every group of managers and told them the same story," he said, "and it is to this day the same thing I tell all our new managers. I talk about how the entire time I've been in management, nobody's ever come to me and asked for more accountability. They'll ask for more authority and they'll ask for more responsibility, but they never want to be held more accountable." He tells his people that accountability is especially important in hospital care because the business can be so unpredictable. While it would be easy for management to throw up its hands, feeling no control over outcomes, Van Gorder urges his managers to do the opposite. "I said this is a tough environment and there are things we can't predict," he said. "But we will accept no excuses for not performing, because we establish our own budget, and when we do that, we are also making a promise that we're going to achieve it."

How does Van Gorder define accountability? "You can miss your quarterly targets once, but you won't be here to miss them twice. That might sound pretty extreme, but I've never had to fire anybody because of it."

As an example, he told me about "Tom," a manager who was running Mercy Hospital San Diego, a very tough hospital to manage. "He could have one trauma case that comes in that costs us over a million dollars with no reimbursement whatsoever," Van Gorder said. Yet a few years back, when Mercy had a very good year financially and earned several quality awards, Tom told Van Gorder he wanted to try for the Baldrige Quality award, which can often be a punishing process. Van Gorder recalled what happened:

> [I told him,] "Tom, be really careful here—I'm worried about you taking your eye off the ball if you're chasing awards. You know my philosophy; I won't tell you you can't do it. You'll get a pat on the back if you win the Baldrige Award. Above all, though, you've got to hit your targets." He said, "Yeah, yeah, Chris, I know and I'll hit all my targets. Don't worry about that." Well, sure enough, they took their eye off the ball, and they started falling short in their monthly earnings. So I brought him in after some of our monthly operating reviews, warned him to get focused because he's in danger of missing his quarterly targets.

At the end of the year, Tom indeed missed those targets. "I said, 'Tom, you know what our philosophy is. What's going to happen now? I love you, big guy. I know your wife and your kids. This is going to break my heart, but if I don't act now, nobody's ever going to believe me again. You've violated our trust by not hitting our targets.'" Van Gorder reminded Tom of his rule and told him that if he wasn't on target within three months, Van Gorder would have to replace him. "You missed your one," Van Gorder told Tom. "You won't be here to miss them twice. You're going to be gone in three months if you're not on target."

Van Gorder made it clear to Tom that he, Tom, would be held responsible for the outcome of his actions. By making Tom aware of his own sense of agency, Van Gorder was allowing him to make the changes necessary to fix the problem. Still, the executive didn't leave

Tom out in the storm alone. He made sure Tom had extra support from the company's project management office and an internal consultant. He told Tom, "I'm even going to help you by having you come in front of the finance committee every month and explain where you are." Tom got back on budget and has never fallen off since that time.

A workforce's sense of agency is a critical determinant of its effectiveness. Van Gorder showed how a leader can teach a mind-set that perceives a higher level of control and responsibility over outcomes. Notice how he didn't fire anyone to do so—he was able to execute this change through his own express expectations of his people and the behaviors reinforced through performance reviews.

What Low Sense of Agency Looks Like

Compare Van Gorder's story with that of "Jeremy," a division president in a large medical-devices company. Jeremy was being groomed for possible promotion to the CEO role. His past success in commercializing products and executing their successful launch had dramatically raised his profile in the company. He had come to be seen as a possible successor to the CEO, and to further stretch him, the company placed him in charge of one of its underperforming divisions. When I met Jeremy, he had been in this new role for two years, and for the first time in his career, he was struggling to deliver. Many around the company had begun to question whether Jeremy had been promoted over his head, and he was feeling tremendous mounting pressure to show dramatic improvements in the division soon or be replaced.

The company's head of human resources, "Diane," asked me to help diagnose why Jeremy was having so much trouble and how best to help him. An in-depth look at his track record, feedback from colleagues, and direct interviews with Jeremy himself revealed that his exceptional marketing talents and intense professional drive had led to an extraordinary level of success very early. But when he had been given a leadership position of dramatically increased scope, his tenure became marked with missteps. This is very normal, as leaders adjusting to a significant increase in responsibility invariably make many mistakes. Those who ultimately excel recognize and own these missteps quickly and use the experiences to grow into their position of elevated authority and increased complexity. But for this learning curve to occur, it is absolutely crucial that they accept their role in these mistakes. If they have a low sense of agency, they cannot, and will fail.

As I got to know Jeremy, it became clear that the exceptional qualities that led to his rapid ascent in the company were indeed impressive. He had a keen sense of market conditions and consumer needs and a knack for connecting the dots in a way that revealed dramatic new market opportunities. These high-profile successes earned him an expansive, well-deserved reputation in the company. But thus far, he had been thriving within divisions that already had well-established world-class operations in place. In Jeremy's new position, he was being asked for the first time to turn a failing team into a strong one. It was an essential test if he was going to be a serious candidate for CEO, and it was one that exposed Jeremy's Achilles' heel.

When I asked Jeremy why he had missed his unit's earning targets every quarter for two years, he immediately deflected responsibility for this critical problem. "This place was a mess when I got here," he said. "I'm doing everything possible to get this thing turned around quickly, but the people here expect miracles. I need more time." Jeremy went on to say he felt he was being judged unfairly by colleagues, that people saw him as a threat and were just waiting for him to fail. "They need to help make me successful, not criticize."

When pushed, Jeremy acknowledged that at least some of his colleagues seemed sincere in wanting him to be successful. But he still blamed his incompetent team for most of the problems. He fired some of those people, but then he found their replacements—people whom he had hired himself—"incompetent" as well.

"You know how it is with first impressions—they can really lie," he said. "I need to have strong individuals willing to challenge me. I can come across as highly intense, and it can silence people. My new hires seemed like they had strong personalities when I first hired them, but once they got here and started working for me, they just weren't strong-willed enough to stand up to me."

Jeremy laid the blame for his division's poor performance on others—even those he himself had fired—showing a very low sense of agency, which is what I explained to him during our feedback session. Until he was able to take ownership of his situation and the central role he played in bringing it about, I told him, he was never going to gain from the critical learning opportunity that had been handed to him with this job. No one was expecting him to flawlessly turn around a situation that was indeed challenging, but Jeremy's problem was that he was showing no upward trajectory that could give his colleagues confidence that he was learning from his mistakes and growing into the job. His low sense of agency was a critical reason.

Peter Drucker used to open many of his lectures to executive audiences by asking, "How many of you have some dead wood in your organizations?" Nearly everyone would raise a hand. Drucker would then ask, "Were they underperformers when you hired them, or did they become so once they started working for you?" This always resulted in a bemused silence.

What made Drucker's question so brilliant was the way he made the people in the audience own their culpability in the performance of their underachievers—that a failure of an employee to perform is in large part due to his or her bosses' failure to find a means for making the employee successful. Drucker's exercise highlights the critical role a high sense of agency plays in successful leadership.

Jeremy revealed his inadequacy in this regard throughout our conversation. But perhaps most damaging were his final comments about needing to surround himself with strong-willed employees. Jeremy assumed it was up to his people to make him successful, not the other way around. No matter how keen Jeremy's commercial instincts and competitive drive were, until he learned how to excel by making others successful, he had no hope of making it as a division president, let alone rising to the company's CEO position.

Unlike Jeremy, leaders with a sense of agency—as well as those who embody an awareness of actual circumstances, as illustrated in chapter 2—recognize where there is room for growth and development in themselves, their companies, and their people. While having an awareness of actual circumstances allows leaders to balance what is known and unknown to prepare for a range of plausible events, a sense of agency takes the catalyst of realistic optimism one step further: viewing those plausible events as being within their own control.

Increasing Your Level of Realistic Optimism

Now that you have taken a look at how the two components of realistic optimism manifest themselves, look back at your answers to the evaluation questions near the beginning of chapter 2 (in the quiz "Evaluating Your Level of Realistic Optimism"). You might have discovered that you lack both an awareness of actual circumstances and a sense of agency. How can you change that?

The human mind uses a variety of defense mechanisms that help it to manage anxiety. These processes are normal and even healthy ways of calming ourselves in a world that poses a potentially paralyzing number of risks and uncertainties. Effectively leading a corporation in a turbulent environment, however, demands that you *learn to minimize the ways your mind distorts reality.*

Research into the nature of these defense mechanisms has shown that they happen unconsciously. One of the most useful studies regarding this phenomenon was published in 2003 by scientists Janice Deakin and Steven Cobley, two of the most accomplished psychologists in the study of expert performance. Deakin and Cobley spent several weeks directly observing the practice routines of twenty-four professional figure skaters of both world-class and mediocre skill. The researchers kept a log of the skaters' solitary practice activities, including the amount of time spent in jump attempts, spins, and rest.

When asked to identify the most critical practice activities that led to improved performance, the skaters unanimously cited the practice of jumps and spins as being far and away the most important. Further, the skaters, regardless of skill level, reported that they devoted almost all of their practice time to these elements. However, direct observations showed that although elite skaters did indeed spend the vast majority of their time on spins and jumps (70 percent), the mediocre skaters spent less than half their practice time on these activities. All of the study subjects believed they were putting in comparable effort, but only the elite skaters were actually doing the activities essential to performance improvement.

Jumps and spins are the most difficult of all practice work, entail the most danger and injury, and display the highest rates of frustration and failure. Deakin and Cobley concluded that one of the most essential qualities that enabled elite skaters to attain their superlative skills was their lack of these avoidance behaviors during their practice routines. Therefore, when the mediocre skaters were encouraged to keep a more objective and accurate log of their actual practice activities, they could disrupt their dysfunctional habits of avoidance and improve their performance to much more closely match that of an elite skater.

The same lessons can be applied to business. As described in chapter 2, when Jim Kilts first took the helm of an underperforming Gillette, he immediately recognized a denial of reality as one of the most pervasive problems in the company's previous leadership. "Sales numbers amongst Gillette's product lines were underperforming and missing targets," he explained, "but leadership had never pursued getting daily or even weekly sales reports. They would wait until the end of each month to find out how they were doing, and as a result, they didn't have the detailed, current information that would allow them to take effective corrective action."

The lack of timely sales performance data was one important example of how Gillette's management had failed to become intimately involved with the details of what was actually going on and why the company regularly missed performance targets but had no idea as to why. Kilts finished his story with a stern warning: "There is a strong tendency in people to put off coming to grips with reality. As a leader, you have to do the opposite—aggressively seek out ways in which performance deficiencies are getting hidden and bring those problems out into the open."

So Kilts did just that, instituting a much more aggressive performance measurement system. "Daily sales reports, for example, are a critical tool to helping an organization manage its inventories and reach targets," he said. "But they also make plain for everyone to see who was hustling to meet their numbers and who was slacking. These metrics led to a lot of tough conversations—and, frankly, some people getting fired. But facing the stark reality was what needed to happen if I was going to get this organization moving with the kind of urgency it needed."

Jim Kilts knew that when companies are underperforming, it is often because leadership has allowed people to avoid their most difficult realties. But when he forced the members of his sales group to report their numbers each day, they could no longer hide from deficiencies. Further, increased transparency dramatically improved management's ability to address performance problems. By the end of his tenure, Kilts had transformed Gillette into one of the most admired companies in the consumer product industry. But he credits compelling his people to face the music for making this happen.

"There was this certain disbelief that we could be so bad," Kilts said. "So I had to make them go through this exercise. I spent a lot of time creating teams that benchmarked everybody's cost so there couldn't be any disagreement at the end of the day. They went through a disciplined process with people who were involved in it, along with some management consultants to force the issues. They didn't want to see the problem. But you force them to look at it. You hold up a mirror to an organization and get them to look at it with absolute honesty."

Kilt's successes at Gillette suggest that while avoidance of reality is a common problem, it is not an insurmountable one. To deal with this problem, you need to make time to reflect on your daily work, your leadership, and your company. Are you willing to see and admit your deficiencies, and then to address them? The brief exercise in "How to Address the Avoidance Problem" will put you on the right path.

By becoming more cognizant of critical behavioral habits and the avoidance behaviors they reflect, individuals can more effectively direct meaningful changes to these patterns. This is how awareness of actual circumstances works in parallel with a sense of agency—increases in one facilitate an increase in the other, ultimately resulting in a higher degree of realistic optimism.

Now that you have evaluated yourself on your level of realistic optimism and completed the exercises toward improving your abilities

How to Address the Avoidance Problem

Make a list of the three most critical hurdles to your long-term career goals. For these three hurdles, identify your least favorite activity involved in each hurdle. Keep a daily calendar log recording the amount of time you actually commit to this critical activity.

After one month, add up the total time spent. How much time are you spending working to improve your deficiencies?

Commit to spending more time focusing on these activities next month, again tallying up your time. You will probably find that most people share a dislike for many of these activities, but by directing your effort to improving them, you are likely to change your conduct in a way that will significantly differentiate you from your peers.

in that area, let's turn to the second critical catalyst for realizing potential in yourself and your people in a time of tumult: subservience to purpose.

4

Subservience to Purpose

Affiliations Based on Shared Dedication

While realistic optimism is the catalyst that allows leaders to see and address deficiencies in themselves and the world around them—and thus grow and realize their potential as a result—subservience to purpose gives them the drive to do so. This drive is particularly important in today's world of distractions and the continued melding of home and work life. Leaders who demonstrate subservience to purpose put a particular pursuit—such as their company's mission—ahead of their own comfort. Quite simply, great leaders equate progress toward this goal with emotional satisfaction. They are, ultimately, servants to their company's most noble purpose.

Yet subservience to purpose is more complicated than a blind refusal to engage in work-life balance; it is a deliberate choice that represents the degree of importance leaders assign to their work. This catalyst reveals itself in the presence of two critical attributes: affiliations based on shared dedication and affect tolerance. *Affiliations based on shared dedication* arise from a leader's interest in cultivating relationships that come from working toward a common, noble purpose. A leader shows *affect tolerance* when he or she has the ability to channel intense reactions to recurring setbacks in a way that constructively keeps the organization moving forward.

As with every driver of realizing potential, proficiency in these two attributes requires both skilled mentorship and specialized practice. For many, it may also require making a difficult choice. But without the powerful means for resilience and tenacity inspired by subservience to purpose, manifesting your potential in a world of ongoing obstacles is simply not possible. We will focus on affiliations based on shared dedication in this chapter and on affect tolerance in the next, but before we get started, try testing your own levels of these attributes in "Evaluating Your Level of Subservience to Purpose."

Evaluating Your Level of Subservience to Purpose

You are the head of marketing for a fast-growing technology company that has undergone some struggles among your leadership team. John, the head of sales, and Barbara, the head of manufacturing, have been at odds for several months, and as a confidant of both individuals, you often find yourself caught in the middle. Both John and Barbara are superstar performers and have privately confided in you that they are exploring leaving the company because of this conflict. Despite your encouraging them to do so, neither one has been willing to involve the CEO, who—admittedly—is a very reactive individual whose interventions tend to worsen rather than resolve conflicts.

Not willing to betray either of their confidences, you instead suggest to your CEO that he hire an outside consultant that specializes in team building to help maximize the team's performance. The CEO responds, "Sounds like a useful exercise." The consultant then conducts private, confidential interviews with each team member. During your session with the consultant, you talk with him about the ongoing conflict and how it is reaching a boiling point. He nods and says, "Yes, yes, I understand." You finish feeling very hopeful that this expert will help finally resolve the situation. At the team-building retreat, when the consultant hands out a summary of the key issues he found regarding your team's effectiveness, you are shocked that the interpersonal friction is not even mentioned. In fact, his conclusion clearly states that your team is functioning at a very high level.

With this scenario in mind, please take no more than one minute to answer all four of the following questions:

1. Which of the following most closely matches your likely response to this situation?

   a. I would immediately ask the consultant for a private moment, during which I would then ask for an explanation of his report's total omission of the costly interpersonal conflict within the team.

   b. I would trust the consultant's expert opinion and hope the situation between John and Barbara improves over the coming months.

2. John is sitting next to you in this meeting. You lean over and whisper to him that you'll have to speak up—the conflict with Barbara needs to be addressed. He responds, "I told you

about my conflict with Barbara in confidence. Doesn't loyalty mean anything to you?" How do you respond?

   a. I would explain to John that your loyalty to both him and the team is very much intact and that this was a good-faith attempt to balance my loyalty to both.

   b. I would assure John that I had not betrayed him.

3. During this phase of the retreat, the CEO looks at you and says, "Looks like this exercise is going to be one hell of a waste of time. Nice suggestion." What do you do?

   a. I'd respond that there are too many important issues that are being avoided within this team that were threatening our performance, and that it was time to address them.

   b. I'd say, "I'm sorry if this was a bad idea, although my intentions were to help the team."

4. The consultant turns to you and says, "I understand this exercise was your idea. What led you to suggest it?" Which most closely mirrors your response?

   a. "I believe we as a group need to find better ways to constructively resolve conflict with one another."

   b. "My friendships with everyone on this team are important to me. I thought we could all benefit from stronger bonds with one another."

For these four questions, the more times you answered "a," the higher your level of subservience to purpose, and therefore the higher your overall level of realizing potential is likely to be.

Each question is designed to measure one of the two components that comprise subservience to purpose. Questions 1 and 3 determine whether you can tolerate uncomfortable affects in order to achieve a broader, more meaningful outcome. Questions 2 and 4 determine how much your affiliations are based on a shared dedication to the group's goals; these questions show whether you view agreeable relations with colleagues as more important than potential friction.

The Unique Nature of Great Leaders' Work Relationships

The work relationships of masterful leaders are characterized by a shared dedication to a noble purpose. What most distinguishes these relationships is that they are *not* based on shared hobbies, a mutual sense of humor, or common backgrounds—things that determine the closeness of most relationships (though having some of these shared interests, of course, does not preclude this kind of affiliation). This is not to suggest that effective leaders are cold or uninterested in forming strong, intimate connections with others. Rather, because gratification derived from purposeful work is so dominant in their psychology, they naturally relate with others who share this perspective. In fact, masters of realizing potential insist on surrounding themselves with coworkers who share this dedication. Leaders who do not are invariably driven out of their teams.

This chapter will explore how the best leaders form these kinds of affiliations that are based on loyalty and camaraderie, including frank performance feedback. It will also examine what these affiliations look like in practice—and what they don't look like.

A New Definition of Loyalty

When affiliations are based on shared dedication, the concept of loyalty among team members becomes redefined: people's level of dedication toward the mission of the enterprise is paramount, rather than their dedication to each other. Inevitably, teams working together tend to develop very strong bonds. But the feelings that result are profoundly influenced by a dominating desire to further the organization's objectives. Miles White, the chairman and CEO of Abbott Laboratories. for more than a decade, talked to me about how he manages the personal loyalties that develop over time with his people, while still maintaining a demand for top performance: "Your first obligation comes back to the enterprise. Managers that are too sympathetic or too accommodating to colleagues out of friendship or affection are ineffective. The fact is that when it comes to the toughest personnel decisions, leadership can be a lonely job."[1]

For example, White once had to retire one of his closest friends, someone White himself had actually worked for when he first came to Abbott. "I had to tell him it was time because things weren't going well, and that was hard, but it had to be done," he said. "To his credit, he made it easy. He knew it was time for him to move on, and we've remained good friends." But White says personal relationships are sometimes a casualty of the job, and leaders must accept that. "My closest team members here kid me about what they call BIF, Blunt Immediate Feedback. I'm the master of BIF," he said, laughing. "They know I'm very direct. I have to be careful that when I deliver an assessment about a given situation . . . I don't crush their feelings. But being straight with them is at the core of our success in working together. They're loyal to me, but it's not a personal loyalty—it's more of a professional loyalty. We definitely have fun together, but at the end of the day, they all know I have to hold them accountable professionally."

It would be inaccurate to suggest that great leaders keep personal feelings out of their work relationships. Professional enterprises occupy the lion's share of their time, energy, and passion. The relationships they form with their colleagues can be very close. But what is unique about these affiliations is that subservience to purpose determines who they bond most closely with in their professional relationships. The level of respect leaders feel for the other's skills and mutual admiration for the intensity of their shared pursuits is central.

This unique aspect of work affiliations relates to the issue of how masterful leaders, especially CEOs, are perceived by others. There is a common misconception that great CEOs are extremely independent people who form only detached, purely professional relationships with their colleagues. For example, when I spoke to a president of a large publishing house, she was surprised by my use of the words "humanity" and "CEO" in the same sentence. She said she assumed that her CEO, and CEOs in general, were "the least self-aware human beings around. They just don't care what other people think about them. I mean, in order to make the tough decisions, they can't get close to people. That's what makes it such a lonely job. In fact, it seems like a kind of depressing job."

This executive's statements were a great illustration of just how mysterious the real life of a CEO often is. In reality, CEOs have told me they think the job is one of the most rewarding paths anyone can be fortunate enough to earn. I don't know a single CEO who regrets having the position. And while CEOs do bear a wide breadth of responsibility, which brings with it a sometimes isolating burden, they are hardly lonely people. Great leaders are not disconnected from the people whom they work with—just the opposite: they demonstrate deep caring for the people who report to them, as Rick Lenny, retired chairman and CEO of The Hershey Company, made clear during our conversation.

"There was a sense from my team that I had to put their feet to the fire, but they also knew I was putting my own feet to the fire," Lenny told me. "And there can be the times where a team member isn't doing his or her job and you have to have the tough conversation. Unfortunately, even after these conversations, a change has to be made, and that's very hard all around. But having strong relationships with your people is worth this potential outcome. They may not be your closest connections in your life, but having a strong personal relationship in addition to a professional relationship—that's worth the risk of what you might have to do down the road." He added that friendship within professional relationships has an added bonus: "that extra ten percent the person gives because of the closeness and the sense of responsibility it inspires."

Affiliations among team members can be stronger than you might expect—even rivaling the kind of accountability family members share. "With a team, there's a level of accountability to the other team members that I don't think holds in a family," Lenny said. "A level of respect, a level of trust to a fellow team member. You are chosen to be part of a team, and you have to hold up your end of the bargain to ensure the team's success. I think it's a higher level of accountability."

Even though their affiliations with colleagues are strongly focused on mutual accountability, CEOs form close relationships with their direct reports, and this mutual sense of commitment is an important part of what facilitates the heightened productivity of their teams. Peak performance cannot be sustained without the camaraderie that comes from an intense, mutual dedication toward a common purpose, and great leaders form teams that generate it. Frank performance feedback is another element found at the heart of relentless leadership, and it is key to building organizational excellence.

Larry Bossidy, the retired Honeywell chairman and CEO whom we met in the introduction, spoke about his "selfish reasons" for giving useful improvement feedback to direct reports: "I could be more successful myself by virtue of training, educating, and developing others. So let's not make this out to be some benevolent act on my part. But it's true, one of the things that used to drive me nuts was to look at personnel appraisals that have been done in a neutered way. They didn't specify nearly enough about what the strengths of the individual were and particularly what the development needs were. So they didn't give people a chance to improve themselves. That lack of feedback robs people of one of the most important reasons they have for coming to work."[2]

What Affiliations Based on Shared Dedication Look Like

Ralph Larsen, during his thirteen years as chairman and CEO of Johnson & Johnson, provides a tangible example of the effects of gathering a team that collectively values the noble mission of the company as the most important driver of the members' connection to one another. In doing so, he built a team with a shared sense of dedication toward this purpose. The result? A stronger sense of team trust based on a common set of values. But Larsen also told me how shared dedication has helped his people pursue their highest potential amid the intense pressure that defines today's market.

"My primary responsibility as a leader was to create an environment that brought the best out of my people," he said. "I don't think you can separate the issue of mentorship and leadership. And I found that the most effective form of mentorship was that I would be blunt when I had to be blunt, but the tone was one of encouragement. If I had to sit down and give somebody a performance review, I absolutely owed it to them to point out things that they didn't realize was a shortcoming." Indeed, Larsen described those developmental conversations that focused on making people improve as "the heart of my job."[3]

But while it's one thing to briefly maintain your affiliations that are based on shared dedication, how do you sustain that kind of subservience to purpose among people in the same company over the long haul, year after year? Larsen did it by reminding his people that they worked for a company that was "one of the finest organizations in the world, making great products—products that heal, cure, and make people feel better," he said. "I always considered it a great privilege to work for Johnson & Johnson doing what I was doing. We were making products that saved lives, from babies to old folks. I had great responsibility. But it was also a wonderful way to spend my life, working with great people, honest people—people who I would turn my family over to."

Even so, as his authority at Johnson & Johnson grew and changed during his thirty years at the company, his affiliations evolved as well:

I think when you talk about loyalty, you take the personal out of it. Loyalty is to the cause, loyalty to the company. My wife and I started as a young married couple at twenty-one, twenty-two, years of age, and we would have colleagues who became friends and came over for dinner. But then as time went on and our responsibilities changed, those friendships dimmed and we no longer had colleagues over for dinner. You might do that once every year, but they were not my golfing partners or dinner companions. I think it's very dangerous to mix friendships and business relationships. Yes, loyalty was important to me. But it was loyalty to the mission, loyalty to the job we had to do, to the company and its mission, which happens to be saving lives.

The dedication Larsen's team members felt toward their company's noble mission created a powerful roadmap for how they would relate to one another. Their commitment to this value system ensured a strong, shared bond: they would drive one another to facilitate their collective goals ahead of other competing interests for their energy or focus.

Note that this has nothing to do with hierarchy or organization charts. Time and again, the intense level of shared dedication to the noble mission of these organizations is reflected in the reduced degree to which employees defer to differences in positional authority. Such hierarchical distinctions are secondary to the overarching value system that considers the company's noble missions its most important function.

"I used to joke that one of the reasons I couldn't wreck Johnson & Johnson as CEO is I had thirteen executive committee members that were very different from me and very empowered," Larsen said. "But it was not really a joke. If I decided we were going to do something crazy and I was just plain wrong, they wouldn't do it. They'd lock me in a closet and nail the door shut and not let me out until I had come to my senses." Larsen said this took a lot of the pressure off him, knowing that he'd helped to build a team that would ensure that he wouldn't do something stupid.

"There was one time when we were about to do a deal, and the deal looked awfully good," he said. "And one of my team members came into my office looking upset. So I shut the door. He says, 'You know, I've never said this to you before, but you are not going to do this deal. You will do this deal over my dead body. I don't trust the people. I don't like the smell of it.'" Larsen turned down the deal and later learned from a competitor who did take the deal that it was a nightmare. "So we missed that bullet, and it was because one of my guys cared so much about our company that he wouldn't let me make the mistake."

In working effectively with his people, Larsen formed relationships in which he and others considered the needs of the company paramount. With this sense of shared dedication, Larsen and his people could address those needs, even if it meant causing friction with one another. Constructive conflict is essential to a team's success; without it, you cannot arrive at the best answer to a problem. And constructive conflict is invigorating, because it reinforces what you've all come together to do, which is to cooperate and drive one another toward a higher purpose. Relationships based on this collective dedication enable you to always come back to your base commitment, your shared purpose—most importantly during times of conflict—that above all brings people together and holds them together.

Any functional relationship requires trust and honesty, even if that means uncomfortable moments. In fact, it is within the most challenging, difficult moments that a higher sense of regard is made possible. By navigating these difficult moments together successfully, you create a higher degree of faith in the resiliency of the relationship.

Traps to Avoid in Work Affiliations

"Craig" was a utility company CEO who was struggling to achieve the expected efficiencies from a large acquisition. As one of Craig's board members put it, "Craig is one of those guys that if you don't get along with him, there's probably something wrong with *you*." And indeed, Craig was extremely likable and friendly. But his inability to build affiliations specifically based on shared dedication was also destroying his effectiveness as CEO.

While Craig had created an intense sense of loyalty from his people, he also had an extremely difficult time managing conflict. This became most apparent after the acquisition. Craig failed to clearly delineate the roles and responsibilities of two of his direct reports, which resulted in a costly turf battle between their departments. One of the division presidents, "Steve," who was at the center of the dispute, explained, "Craig is such a terrific guy. But with conflict, he doesn't seem to see it, or he'll ignore it and hope it will work itself out somehow. We just went through the merger, and one of the key areas that affect my business is IT. In the operating groups, we are losing our autonomy—we can no longer set our own budget. Now it goes through IT. We are going through a process that our CIO [chief information officer] developed. I went to Craig and told him that if this is going to work, I need to be involved in shaping this process because it involves me critically." He asked Craig to be straight with him: if Steve was no longer going to have a voice, he needed to know that.

But Craig was neither straight with Steve, nor straight with the CIO, Joe, when he came to meet with Craig. As Steve told me, "Joe goes to Craig and tells him something that involves me as an operating person, but Craig doesn't correct him for going around me. I've told Craig that Joe needs to come to me. But Craig isn't correcting political behavior in this way. The CIO then presented our proposed projects to the leadership committee in a way that made one of our critical initiatives seem unappealing." Craig's openness to talk with anyone undermines the structure that he should be defending—and that should be everyone's shared interest.

I sat down with Craig to summarize my findings—that he needed to show more willingness to address conflict and sensitive interpersonal issues among his team members. But Craig insisted on remaining quiet. "It's not that I won't deal with it, but sometimes it's better to let certain things amongst team members pass," he said. I told him that I agreed with him—about some instances. But when conflicts between subordinates are recurring and can be traced to a fundamental lack of clear differentiation in the responsibilities of each participant, the leader needs to step in.

Craig disagreed, asking instead, "What else do you have for me?" I tried to bring him back to the topic at hand, especially how his lack of clear direction and help to his team was affecting his people's ability to integrate the present merger. I told him that the core root of failure of so many mergers and acquisitions is the lack of clarity regarding the roles and responsibilities of the merged staffs—which was exactly what was happening among his people.

As Craig continued to assert that "sometimes it's just better to let a conflict go than start an argument," it grew ever more clear that he was avoiding the issue because he did not want to come into conflict with his colleagues. He was putting his affiliations above the shared dedication that really should have been dictating them. But because he telegraphed to his team how uncomfortable these kinds of conversations made him, his people were encouraged to avoid confrontations, as he did. As a consequence, people were not having these important conversations with each other. The result was a big role-clarification problem that was still festering two years after the merger and showing no sign of being addressed.

Craig refused to engage me in any substantive way after that. He did not lose his job (as head of a large, regulated public utility, he would have a hard time getting fired). Because of this high job security and conflict-avoidance atmosphere of public utilities, politics, festering performance issues, and other dysfunction are common in this industry. It's a unionized workforce with regulated pricing and a fixed, captive market. Keeping the peace among the groups was a useful tool. But Craig's insistence on doing so at the expense of performance was clearly hurting the company's shareholders and profits. His conflict-avoidance problems kept him from being as effective as he could be, yet he was competent enough despite this problem, given the unique demands of his industry.

———————

In this chapter, we have looked at the role that affiliations based on shared dedication play in a leader's subservience to purpose. If you as a leader do not foster relationships among your colleagues—and if those relationships are not based on a shared purpose—then you will be unable to realize your own potential, and your people will ultimately fail as well. Let's now turn to the second characteristic of subservience to purpose: affect tolerance.

5

Subservience to Purpose

Affect Tolerance

I t's not unusual for leaders to experience a full range of emotional reactions every day—and these include anxiety, loneliness, frustration, and a sense of grandiosity, or self-importance. That is only more the case in today's fast-paced environment. Leaders who are subservient to a purpose can channel the tough feelings triggered in this kind of environment in a way that stimulates rather than hinders progress. Psychologists call this *affect tolerance,* or the ability to channel intense reactions to recurring setbacks in a way that not only avoids hampering you, but also constructively keeps you and your organization moving forward toward maximum potential.

This chapter shows how affect tolerance can help aspiring leaders manage their feelings so that they and their people can progress. It looks at how leaders' expression of emotions can negatively affect their teams and how staying focused can help leaders steer clear of the particularly insidious problem of grandiosity. We will also see illustrations of what affect tolerance looks like and what it doesn't look like. The chapter's final section provides some thoughts and an exercise for improving your overall ability to remain subservient to a higher purpose.

Staying Afloat Under Extreme Adversity

Let's begin with a story of how one leader stayed focused under the most forbidding of circumstances. In April 1996, Jim McNulty was asked to take over as CEO of Parsons Corporation a few days after his boss, Len Pieroni, died in an airplane crash in the Adriatic Sea. The accident also took the lives of U.S. Secretary of Commerce Ronald Brown and thirty-three other executives.

"They called me in and offered me the job," McNulty recounted. "This was a shock—I had only been a division president for three months. All of us were still stunned about what had happened. And I was thrown in the deep end. I had no background in finance. This was a big deal because I did not yet understand how precarious Parsons' finances could become."[1] One Sunday afternoon a few months later, McNulty learned about Parsons' recurring struggles with cash. "My wife and I were coming home from the funeral of the wife of a project manager when I got a call from our CFO," he said. "He told me we didn't have enough cash to make payroll. I asked him how that was possible, and he explained that there had been an unanticipated delay in payment from several of our customers."

At this point, not only did McNulty have to unexpectedly handle his transition into the role of CEO and the tragic death of his former boss and colleague, but he was immediately forced to deal with a drastic fiscal crisis that threatened the company's solvency. One could easily imagine how overwhelming the pressure of this situation felt, especially his getting the news while driving home from the funeral of an employee's spouse. But a CEO today must be able to solve difficult problems under exactly this kind of pressure, while under emotional fire from all angles. What McNulty did next illustrates how his ability to tolerate such a stressful situation enabled him to realize his own potential and that of his people.

"First, I got on the phone with our bankers to arrange for an extension of our credit line," he told me. "Then I started to dig into things and found out that cash-flow issues had been a perennial problem at the company. That had to change. But keeping the company solvent required making some very unpopular moves. It meant totally changing how we dealt with cash." For instance, Parsons had always paid a generous Christmas cash dividend to all employees. But in a cash-strapped business, McNulty had to eliminate the dividend and contend with people's unhappiness.

"I walked in one morning, and there was a note on my office door with one word on it," he said. "I'll let you guess what that word was, but it wasn't flattering. I was not real popular." Why McNulty took such a risk, particularly when he was still trying to gain people's confidence as their new CEO, illustrates the height of affect tolerance. He did it, he said, "because it was the right thing for the business. It allowed us the financial stability and flexibility that would allow us to grow and make some critical acquisitions." By staying focused on the steps necessary to keep the company solvent and significantly improving its prospects for avoiding these problems in the future, McNulty improved the business's viability even during a time of distress.

McNulty's trials were far from over, and his profound commitment to the progress of the enterprise continued to be tested. At one point, the company was in the midst of making a major acquisition when the unthinkable occurred: one of his employees was kidnapped while he was working in the Philippines. Ultimately, McNulty was able to negotiate for his release. But, he told me, "this was one of the most difficult events of my tenure. It was extremely stressful. But people were looking to me for reassurance and guidance. And it's my job to give it, regardless of how I might be feeling inside."

Jim McNulty's experience illustrates the affect tolerance one must manage when in charge of a large global enterprise in today's economy. Intense emotional reactions to such circumstances are inevitable. This is why a leader's deeply held conviction in the importance of his or her work is so essential. If you are to maintain an ongoing determination in the face of such challenges, you must believe that what you're doing will make a meaningful, positive contribution. Such an attitude gives you the affect tolerance you need to channel these emotions into actions that ensure progress.

Managing Emotions Constructively to Realize Potential

Most people find their progress dramatically slowed by their emotional reactions when confronting forbidding situations. The great leaders we have studied have learned how to manage these feelings in a way that allows them to continue making progress, even during times of the most extreme pressure.

This outward calm and focus in the face of stressors not only helps individual leaders rise to their best achievements, but also shows their people how to do the same. Raymond Milchovich, CEO of Foster Wheeler, faced forbidding challenges while keeping his team moving constructively to address threats to their organization's survival. Milchovich joined Foster Wheeler when the hundred-year-old company was nearly bankrupt, and he faced an additional hurdle: although he'd come from a manufacturing background, he was being asked to save an engineering and construction company.

"During the first handful of months," Milchovich told me, "the extent of the problems shocked even me." To renegotiate the company's debts on a credible business plan, Milchovich needed to know the true depth of the issues. "It took me at least two years to get through the issues that I discovered just to believe that I had found the bottom."[2]

Milchovich's experience offers a unique window into what it's like to manage a severe organizational crisis. It's also a great example of how someone can use the pressure of a situation to invigorate his or her own efforts and the team's energy.

"I started on the twenty-first of October," Milchovich recalled. "On December third, we were down to three million dollars of domestic cash. Now, there's a big flywheel running, and we are literally almost out of money. Just for some perspective, today we have more than one billion dollars of liquid cash on the balance sheet." The company almost ran out of money three times during those early years, but Milchovich was rapidly putting in controls to conserve cash.

The problem was that his senior team had been in place since before he arrived, and it "didn't believe the building was burning," in Milchovich's words. "So, the first thing I had to do was create the awareness that we had a significant problem here. I had to be very, very provocative all the time, trying to create a level of urgency that this thing's ready to come apart. So a big part of this was rapidly attempting to drive a stake through the heart of the old culture. It was a daunting task, and the hell of it was that I was alone." Ultimately, Milchovich replaced the entire senior team with lower-level managers "who could get it"—all while the company was running out of cash.

Throughout the crisis, Milchovich also maintained his fortitude and enthusiasm for the challenge. The emotions he experienced allowed him to rise to a higher plane of activity. "I was fifty-one or fifty-two when I came in," he said. "I figured this was it for me. This was either going to work or it wasn't. And one thing I've never had trouble with: when it gets tough, I can find another gear. I just refuse to lose, and we worked seven days a week. When the leader does that, it gives energy and oxygen to the rest of the organization, because I wasn't asking anyone to do anything that I wasn't doing."

It helped that the new senior team that he'd found fully grasped the situation. "These people always knew things were a mess," he said. "They just weren't quite sure what they could do about it. It was as if I'd removed a layer of management that was suffocating these people and gave them oxygen." With the new team in place, the company began to gain momentum. It was able to build on its own understanding of the urgency of the situation, and following Milchovich's example, it used this energy to make an extraordinary effort.

Milchovich also made a point of including everyone in the discussions. "I listen to others," he said. "I don't care whose idea it is." He told me his team did its best work when it debated issues and tried to capture its collective thinking. Milchovich's practice of sharing the burden of the challenge with his team members in a way that emphasized each of their roles in ensuring their survival allowed him to draw the maximum collective effort from the group. By creating a sense of shared burden, he intensified the group's cohesion and cooperative spirit. In the most urgent, high-pressured situations, only by sharing our fears and mutual dependence can we hope to persevere. And this results as a positive side-effect, a team that builds trust and closeness in the knowledge that it can face and overcome new challenges.

Incidentally, Milchovich also cited his relationship with his wife, whom he has known since he was sixteen, as key. "I'm blessed with a wife that I've been with all my life. Our priorities are aligned, and when I need to do what I need to do, I get a hundred percent support and so all I have to do is go do it." The strain of leading an organization through a period of crisis is unavoidable. Milchovich's openness about his stable, nurturing relationship with his wife provides insight into the critical, restorative nature of a healthy home life and its role in fortifying a leader's affect tolerance.

Milchovich's approach offers a critical lesson: that maximum, ongoing effort requires shared ownership of the problem. Ultimately, however, even in an environment where the team collectively discusses solutions, the CEO is still considered the final arbiter. To manage that kind of stress, especially amid a long-lived crisis, Milchovich told me, you need trusting relationships: "I think you have to have people you can talk to. I mean, you have to find trusted colleagues that you can just talk one-on-one about things that are troubling you, because I think people that try to hold it all in and do it all themselves—or not expose themselves because they don't want to look weak—I just don't think that works. I don't think that's the essence of good leadership."

By managing his fears and vulnerabilities in a constructive way, Milchovich was able to maintain an ongoing focus on facilitating the maximum collective effort from his team despite an environment of extraordinary stress. But to do so—to prevent the pressure of being the one ultimately responsible for the company's success or failure from clouding his judgment—he channeled his needs for support and reassurance in a way that did not distract his people. He relied on a stable, supportive spouse as well as a few trusted colleagues. In doing so, Milchovich modeled how an individual can sustain an extraordinary level of focus even during long periods of struggle by managing his emotional needs constructively.

How Leaders' Expressions of Emotion Affect Teams and Companies

One of the most critical tasks for leaders operating within a stressful environment is to channel their emotions and reactions in a way that does not hinder their people's progress. In order to discipline yourself for the greater good of the company in this way, you first need to understand the outsized effect that your emotional behaviors have on your people.

My interaction with "Jeffrey," the soon-to-be CEO of an industrial company, provides a perfect example of the landmines that await leaders who ignore the effects of their emotional behavior. It was a Friday afternoon, and I was sitting in a conference room at the company headquarters, waiting to give him feedback. The night before, I had sent him a summary of my conclusions, including some detailed feedback about areas he needed to improve. Jeffrey arrived seeming visibly agitated, giving me little more than a cursory hello and handshake before he sat down across from me. I asked if he'd had a chance to read the report I sent him, and he replied that he had.

Then I said, "You seem upset. Did you have something more immediate that you wanted to talk about?" After a few minutes of hostile silence, Jeffrey replied in a frustrated tone, "This report certainly doesn't sound like it's describing someone qualified to be CEO."

I could understand Jeffrey's reaction. For the past twenty-five years, he had given everything to this company. He had moved his family all over the world, never hesitating to go wherever the company needed him to be. He wouldn't even miss work the day his father died. Jeffrey loved the company, believed in it, and was willing to sacrifice everything for it.

Jeffrey had been identified early in his career as having CEO potential, and had been given a diversity of work assignments around the company to prepare and test him. He had attacked every assignment with a voracious determination to succeed and had dramatically improved the function of every area he touched. His effectiveness and breadth of experience made him the obvious choice as the next CEO, but before officially naming him, the board wanted an outsider to give Jeffrey counsel that would help him make the transition more successfully.

I asked Jeffrey which part he thought made him sound unqualified. He replied that the part that said he wasn't open to the ideas and feedback of others was "inaccurate and unfair." I observed aloud that in fact, he was demonstrating this problem in front of me that very moment. Rather than engaging in an open inquiry about how others could have arrived at what he thought was a misperception of him, he appeared much more interested in disputing its validity.

Jeffrey sat forward and, in a lowered voice, almost growled his response: "Well, Justin," he said, "that's just bullshit. I'm defending myself because the board saw these comments, too. This isn't just about my development—it's also about whether or not I'm qualified to be CEO. And a comment like that makes it sound like I'm not."

I paused a beat to allow the highly aggressive energy in his response to dissipate a bit before I explained that this was a process to help ensure his success as he moved into the CEO role—it wasn't about deciding whether or not he would be taking that position. "And the way you are responding in this moment is exactly what you most need to work on," I said. "I'm not talking about the fact that you get frustrated—who wouldn't?—but it's how you manage your frustration that is important."

While certainly Jeffrey needed to learn how to accept and respond to criticism, at the crux of the problem was his inability to manage his feelings of frustration or anger when he was criticized. In this instance, Jeffrey was extremely anxious about the board's upcoming announcement, and his fear of failure was creating his feelings of vulnerability. The stress of these emotions was expressed in his palpably intense tone toward me—an individual he considered an instrumental figure responsible for creating this stress. While his reaction to the uncertainty of his circumstance was understandable, the way he was expressing it was unacceptable.

The problem was that this response was mirrored in the way he worked and received feedback from his colleagues, and this reactivity to setbacks risked creating a powerful distraction for his employees. I told Jeffrey that I had talked to people who had worked with him for more than twenty years. "They told me that when you think someone says something ill-considered in a meeting, you roll your eyes," I said. "When you think time is being wasted, you sigh heavily and lean back in your chair. When you disagree, your questions have a sharp tone that makes people feel interrogated. This is why people find you 'silencing.' Right now, you're frustrated. You think you've been wrongly accused. But the way you expressed your frustration is a problem. The growling tone. The look of anger. A CEO simply can't do that."

Jeffrey's urge to vent placed his own needs above the higher goal of the company's productivity, since the energy of his temper would invariably hinder his employees' ability to do their work. Jeffrey sat in silence for a moment. When he responded, his tone was already slightly more measured.

"It's not like no one's told me this before. [The current CEO] has told me this many times," Jeffrey said. "But I'm not sure what the big deal is. I'm just being honest, and I would expect people to be able to handle that."

As I told him that day, while there was nothing wrong with honesty, candor needs to be tempered with an awareness of the *outsized effect a CEO's behavior has on others because of the executive's positional authority.* Our study had clearly revealed that Jeffrey could say something in a meeting or write a one-liner e-mail that just decimated people.

Words, tones, and body language all transmit messages to subordinates and affect people's sense of competence, not to mention their positional status and daily comfort. These are the central building blocks of a person's identity. Leaders like Jeffrey must keep this in mind when they find themselves having an intense reaction. How they express strong emotions in front of others must take into account the outsized effect these expressions can have on people rightly or wrongly in the line of fire.

As a leader in today's economy, you inevitably experience moments of intense frustration, aggravation, and even dejection. But you must be able to check any impulses to unleash these potentially disruptive reactions on your team. This is not to say that you must avoid authentic reactions, but you must temper the intensity of these responses with the awareness of the unequal power dynamics you share with your team. A leader's comments invariably have a magnified impact, and if you lead in an environment that guarantees ongoing obstacles and setbacks, you must remain conscious of how the intensity of your most reactive moments will reverberate through your workforce. During these moments, you have to place the needs of the organization and its people above your own.

Jeffrey eventually did improve as a leader. But this brings us back to an earlier point, that every great leader is still human and has "selves" that are not his or her best, selves that particular contexts can cause to emerge and dominate this person. The key is to illuminate for the individual the circumstances that cause these dysfunctional selves to emerge and find ways to manage them. Active, in-the-moment feedback about when Jeffrey's loss of temper was manifesting helped him slowly but surely bring this under control. He needed to share with his team his struggle with his temper and ask people to give him feedback when he crossed the line in a way that silenced them. He did this, and he is the CEO today—an extraordinarily successful one.

We all have human imperfections and vulnerabilities that can appear, given the right triggers. It is our responsibility to become aware of what these triggers are and grow as individuals to bring them more under control as we mature. This ongoing process is part of realizing our potential as leaders, but it is a growth that lasts a lifetime.

The Siren Song of
Grandiosity

One of the most destructive things about positions of authority, and the power that comes with them, is how authority can induce in people an outsized feeling of *grandiosity,* or self-importance. To some degree, all of us have a rush when we first feel the profound effect our positional authority can have on the behaviors of people reporting to us. This reaction is perfectly normal and, in fact, inevitable. But it is essential that leaders remain conscious of this sense of grandiosity when it surfaces and ensure that it does not dominate their behaviors, especially in times of duress. Otherwise, they will have trouble staying focused on their higher purpose and reaching their maximal potential.

This time, we'll turn to a non-business figure to illustrate the problems with grandiosity. It was November 2, 2007, and Senator Barack Obama had shocked everyone, taking an insurmountable lead in the U.S. Democratic Party presidential primary over the heavily favored Senator Hillary Clinton. Victory after victory at the polls, adulations from millions of admirers, and a very plausible shot at becoming the most powerful person in the world—it was in the midst of these events that he rose to make a speech to an African American audience at a church in Manning, South Carolina.

Appearing pleased and relaxed in front of the welcoming crowd, he quickly went off script and began imitating the call-response cadence of a preacher: "I'm not running to be *vice* president . . . I'm not running to be *secretary* of something or other . . . I was doing just *fine* before I started running for president! I'm a United States Senator *already.*"[3] The audience, fired up just moments ago, grew silent and uncomfortable. The bravado Obama was exhibiting seemed wrong, inappropriate, particularly in a place of worship. For a man widely recognized for his extraordinary ability to move an audience, he was suddenly missing his cues.

Instead he pressed even further: "Everybody already *knows* me! I already *sold* a lot of books! I don't *need* to run for president to get on television or on the radio. I've *been* on Oprah!" By this point, the crowd was dead silent. As excited as the people had been to come out and celebrate the young senator's success, his breach of decorum, praising his own name so crassly, was simply unacceptable.

Obama had allowed feelings of grandiosity to overcome him, blinding his judgment and creating one of his more embarrassing stumbles on the campaign trail. A human being confronted with intense, ongoing idealization by the public eye can become vulnerable to that—and how it can affect the person's ability to manage his or her own feelings. But it is those feelings that those who display affect tolerance overcome and channel instead into productive action.

The power associated with any position of authority can trigger feelings of grandiosity, a feeling that, if not properly managed, can totally disconnect leaders from the realities around them. In this way, affect tolerance is similar to an awareness of actual circumstances; grandiosity dangerously distorts leaders' understanding of themselves and the world around them. Grandiosity is by its very nature a swelling of a person's self-image into a delusional state of grandeur, and anyone, given the right set of circumstances, is vulnerable to its manifestation.

Chris Van Gorder, CEO of Scripps Health System, has a unique personal history with learning to manage this affect—and attempting to teach that to another leader. Van Gorder was originally recruited to come to Scripps by Stan Pappelbaum, the CEO at the time—an exceptional strategist from whom Van Gorder felt he could learn a lot. But just three months after Van Gorder arrived, Stan was abruptly fired and Van Gorder was named interim CEO.

"Stan was the reason I came to Scripps, but soon after I got here, I realized he was in trouble," Van Gorder told me. "He had such innovative ideas, but he couldn't get anyone to follow him, because he wouldn't listen to any input from his team." In a moment of supreme frustration after Stan had announced a major strategy shift in an executive committee meeting, Van Gorder approached him privately. "He hadn't run the idea by any of us, and I told him his plan didn't make any sense for a lot of reasons. I explained why I felt so strongly, and he responded, 'Well, this is the way I want to do it.' "[4]

Because Van Gorder was convinced that the move would prove disastrous for Stan, he took a chance to try to get through to the CEO. Van Gorder told Stan a story about his time as a police officer, when he was in his early twenties. He recounted his months in training and how stifling that was, and how when training was finally over and he was out on his own, he felt his new sense of power intensely. As he told Stan, "Now you know you're a cop. If there's a hot call, you can go a hundred miles an hour and blow through intersections and nobody's looking over your shoulder. It's amazing how heavy that badge becomes when it's hanging from your shirt."

One night, when Van Gorder was on his way to a burglary in progress, he blew through a red light without his lights and siren on—and just barely missed another police car coming through the green light. "Somehow I hit my brakes, they hit their brakes, and spinning out of control—by the grace of God, we missed each other. And I sat there with my heart pounding almost out of my chest. That was a two-man unit, and they were, to say the least, very unhappy with me. And my God, this aggressive behavior could have killed me, but more important, it could have killed them."

Van Gorder told Stan, "You're feeling a little badge-heavy right now, and you believe that just because you said you know to go this way, everybody's going to follow you. They aren't, and you're going to kill yourself as a CEO and then maybe a whole lot of other people along with you." Stan thanked Van Gorder for his story and stuck to his own plan. When, a few weeks later, Stan's decision blew up in his face, the board fired him. That day, Stan sat down in Van Gorder's office and said, "I crashed my car, didn't I?" Indeed he had. As Van Gorder put it, the badge had gotten really heavy for Stan.

Grandiosity also deals a fatal blow to a leader's ability to help his or her people live up to their potentials, because it causes an elevated level of self-absorption. Within that disconnect, any sense of team is lost, as the group unconsciously gets the sense that its collective efforts are being used to uplift the leader's ego, rather than to pursue a shared goal.

Grandiosity is particularly costly to you as a leader, because its expression unintentionally telegraphs to your subordinates that you believe the group's accomplishments are largely due to your involvement. This is why expressing humility is so important, because when you are humble, you clearly communicate to others that you recognize the critical role each team member plays in contributing to the organization's progress.

Fred Smith, founder, chairman, and CEO of Federal Express, described to me the role humility plays in generating the maximum engagement of a workforce. "Time and again, you see less-gifted teams or athletes beat the more favored entity, simply because they're able to pull forward that discretionary effort—and that comes from good leadership," Fred said. "Leaders can't be self-oriented—their primary focus has to be on the needs of their team. This requires having a great deal of empathy and interest in the people that work for them."[5]

Smith, who started FedEx from scratch, explained that he has continually resisted the temptation to equate the company's extraordinary success with his personal effort, talent, and sacrifices:

As a founder, you must be able to resist any temptation to let the organization become a cult of personality built around you. FedEx isn't about me. When I walk out the door here, this

organization won't miss a beat. That comes from getting competent people really motivated, and in order to do so, you must be
willing to delegate to those people a lot of responsibility—give
them skin in the game. That's the only way to get the discretionary effort we were talking about. It's the only way to win. We
did that from the beginning. All of us shared a big stake in this
business, and each of us had independent decision-making authority that would make a difference.

Smith continuously emphasized just how dependent his success
had been on the efforts of the people who work for him. He refused
the potential reverence he might have received as the face of a company that revolutionized and came to dominate its industry. Instead,
he has always shared credit for the success of the company with his
people, among other things giving them a heavy personal financial
stake in the success of the venture, as well as the decision-making authority that would profoundly affect its success.

If they don't keep their feelings of self-importance in check, leaders
can become completely self-absorbed and isolated from their teams.
These grandiose self-perceptions are fragile; if leaders wish to maintain their sense of self-importance, they must reject any feedback that
contradicts their self-delusion. Because self-absorbed people have a
sort of tunnel vision that focuses on their own superiority, rather than
on any more important goal, their self-absorption is especially costly if
they hold positions of authority. The more successful and praised you
are as a leader, the more vigilant you must be to keep any sense of
grandiosity in check. Although it is only natural to feel self-important
when you are extraordinarily good at something, these feelings pose a
potentially grave threat to your effectiveness as a leader.

Next, let's get a clearer idea of how affect tolerance works in practice with the following two stories—one of a highly focused executive
and one of an executive with low affect tolerance.

High Affect Tolerance: Looking
Duress in the Face

One of the world's most powerful businessmen was looking for an heir to his corporate empire from among his children. With that goal in mind, he declared that he wanted to make his youngest son, whom we'll call "Jeremy," the CEO of one of his larger companies. The announcement brought tremendous press attention about family rivalry and who was the favorite to take over for the aging patriarch. Spokespeople from the national government, fearing that nepotism could endanger the health of one of the country's high-profile, extremely successful corporations, made statements to the press that they had concerns about the move. The resulting outcry caused several board members to hesitate out of fear for their own reputations, and they demanded that an outside evaluator (me) be brought in to evaluate Jeremy.

Unbeknownst to me, during my flight to the corporate headquarters, the situation got even more complicated. The media had gotten hold of this perfect storm of a story: powerful businessman wants to give control of one of the country's crown corporate jewels to his son, a man barely past age thirty. I went from the airport directly to my hotel to clean up and meet with Jan, the consultant that was managing the client relationship. When I sat down across from Jan at my hotel's restaurant, I could see a deep look of concern on her face. Then she handed me the front page of the business section from that morning's newspaper, on which blared the headline "Jeremy to Be Psychoanalyzed by Californian Psychologist."

The article claimed that I was a Jungian therapist who was going to judge Jeremy's relationship to his mother and father and his overall level of neuroticism. Next to the article was a caricature of Jeremy lying on a couch and a Freud-like character sitting opposite him, taking notes. Naturally, the article increased the tension around a situation

developing into a circus-like atmosphere. I was instructed for the dura-
tion of my stay to avoid discussing the project on either my cell or hotel
phone and to avoid communicating about it via e-mail.

I went to meet Jeremy the next day in our local office. I waited in a
room down the hall from the conference room in which we would
meet; outside my door were the normal sounds of a bustling office of
people working in a densely packed floor. There was no need for anyone to tell me when Jeremy had arrived in the conference room.
There was a palpable change of energy and sounds in the office, an
unmistakable buzz of lowered voices all talking at once. As I walked
up the hall to meet Jeremy, I saw heads peeking up over the cubicles,
a final indicator of the absurd level of attention that the situation had
taken.

These were actually the perfect circumstances under which to talk
to Jeremy. He was a young man who had been put in an extraordinarily complex, volatile, highly sensitive situation. Inaccurate sources of
data had potentially predisposed him to be hostile to my approach.
The outcome of our conversation would lead to a decision that would
make public whether or not he was judged capable of living up to his
father's extraordinary expectations of him. Was his father, a historically brilliant evaluator of talent, blinded by his love for his son, as the
board feared, or was his father seeing the very real potential Jeremy
possessed? Precisely because of the high volatility of the situation, I
could not have asked for a better setting in which to find out whether
the young man was ready to handle the chief executive position. Seeing how Jeremy behaved under duress would say a lot about how he
would conduct himself as a leader.

When I walked in, Jeremy stood up and shook my hand, looking
me squarely in the eye. He showed little anxiety, other than watching
me carefully as I put my things down, took my jacket off, and sat. No
sign of shaky hands. No alteration in the cadence or speed of his

speech. Nothing forced or obviously managed about his eye contact. There was tension, of course; he was nervous. But I could already tell that he was far less so than the average human placed in a similar set of circumstances would be. He was tolerating the ambiguity of the situation and his own fears, waiting to see what I was going to ask him, rather than feeding off the press's frenzy and doubting my moves from the get-go.

Throughout our conversation, Jeremy answered my questions in a measured way. While he was willing to have the exchange as it was presented to him, I could tell that he was constantly scanning for ulterior motives. When I asked him a question that lacked clarity, or when he felt I'd misinterpreted something he said, his tone and facial expression exposed an edgy aggressiveness, subtle but unmistakable. His awareness of the circumstances he was in, and what he had to do in order to get the job he badly wanted, was guiding him as he navigated our back and forth. His responses were clear, practical. Tough and somewhat irritable at first, he became more flexible and patient when my reactions to his initial prickliness caused no visible negative judgment in me.

Jeremy was showing an incredibly high level of skill for someone his age (or any age, for that matter) to manage ambiguity, stress, irritation, and yet maintain clarity of thought, purpose, and forward direction. This suggested he was unusually well prepared to manage his reactions to extraordinary pressures on the job. His admirable ability to channel his emotions in a way that maintained progress revealed his capacity for leading others in environments of duress.

Jeremy was, as I reported to the board afterward, everything his father insisted he was—an unmistakable rising star. He ended up as CEO of the company for five years, delivering exceptional results year after year, until he was promoted to an even higher position of authority within his father's company and was announced as the heir apparent to the family empire. This time, there was no controversy about the promotion.

Low Affect Tolerance: Avoiding
Anger at All Costs

While Jeremy was able to manage his emotions and maintain clarity in high-intensity situations, "Harry" was a different story. In some senses, Harry was very good at managing his emotions—too good. Because he could not stand the negative tension that comes from conflict, he avoided it at all costs, letting his fear of conflict cloud his judgment.

Harry was known as an exceptional rainmaker, president of the most profitable division of a global heavy-equipment manufacturer. There was a horserace for the CEO position between Harry and the president of another division, "Timothy." The retiring CEO felt strongly that Harry wasn't right for the job, but the board insisted on doing its own analysis. When I asked the current CEO what his greatest concern about Harry was, he said, "In twenty years, I don't think Harry has ever fired anyone. Some of the people on his team have been incompetent, and getting him to address it is like pulling teeth. I've told him he's got to fix this, but he doesn't. Just drives me nuts."

Harry's other colleagues and subordinates agreed that Harry was indeed almost entirely externally focused. Most worrisome in terms of his potential for taking over the CEO role, none of his team had ever received substantive performance feedback from him. In fact, despite the company's mandate for annual performance reviews, Harry's reviews were always delivered late, and the information was bereft of any significant negative comments.

When I met Harry, he was just as I pictured—warm, easy smile; immaculate, fully bespoke suit; and large, brightly polished gold cufflinks. Talkative, easygoing, he made it fun to spend time with him. He was a terrific storyteller.

After a while, we shifted to talking about his aspirations for the future, and it was clear that Harry very much wanted the CEO job. But given how the CEO role at this company required much more of an operations focus, I was curious about why Harry had not adapted his current position to include a stronger focus on operations, particularly given the repeated feedback from his boss. In fact, Harry told me that he was on the road more than three hundred days per year and left the division's daily operations in the hands of his subordinate, "Gary." I asked Harry to tell me about Gary's strengths and weaknesses, and he replied, "No significant weaknesses. Gary does whatever is asked of him, and does everything well."

When I asked him how often Gary and the rest of his team received feedback, he said, "Whenever they need it. They are terrific, I'm lucky to have them." I told Harry that although it was clear he felt very good about his team, it didn't seem as if he was very involved in the development, even though his CEO had asked him to do more.

Harry became slightly agitated, replying, "Yes, he has an opinion. But I think I'm as involved as I need to be. It's hard to argue with my numbers."

I told Harry that I was curious why he was unresponsive to his boss's feedback, particularly given that he wanted to succeed him in the role. "Do you think the CEO role should have more of an external focus than [the current CEO] gives it?" I asked him.

He stammered, "No, no. I'm not saying that at all. Forgive me if I misspoke. I think [the current CEO] is doing a fantastic job."

Notice that Harry was apologizing for what he feared was my own misinterpretation of his opinion regarding how the CEO should be spending his time. He was taking responsibility for my own possible misunderstanding regarding a critical issue—what Harry thought should be the priorities of the company's CEO. By apologizing for a potential misunderstanding, which if it existed would have been largely my fault, Harry was exposing an overanxiousness to avoid tension between us. Whatever irritation or frustration he felt, he was visibly swallowing it and instead trying to maintain a pleasant relationship between us.

I asked Harry why he hadn't shifted his own practices to be more internally focused. At that, he reddened slightly, his voice becoming a bit more abrupt. "I just haven't needed to," he said, implying that his profitability spoke for itself.

Harry had proven to be tremendously successful growing the business in the Middle East—a very challenging culture for Westerners to adapt to. When I asked Harry about it, he spoke in a more relaxed tone. "Yes, well, that's taken a long time to build," he said. "My competitors don't understand how to do business there. You can't just land, make your presentation, and leave. I go for a week, and the first couple of days are about getting to know your customers and their families. We don't talk business until they are ready to. So we eat lots of four-hour-long meals—my doctor tells me I'm a heart attack waiting to happen, but I just can't resist the food. You should see what they put together over there."

When I reviewed my findings for the board, I explained why Harry avoided giving more constructive development feedback to his people despite recurring criticism from his boss that he needed to do so. Harry could not tolerate the uncomfortable feelings that accompanied difficult conversations and responded by avoiding them. This also stood in the way of Harry's creating a team with affiliations based on shared dedication; instead, his affiliations were based on his own desire to avoid conflict.

Improving Your Level of
Subservience to Purpose

As we've described in the last two chapters, subservience to purpose is more than simply a struggle with work-life balance. It represents a conscious choice to give primacy to your pursuit of a meaningful goal. Fortunately, as with all attributes for realizing potential, subservience to purpose (and its two key aspects, affect tolerance and affiliation based on shared dedication) can be learned.

Take, for instance, one of the most celebrated and replicated studies in developmental psychology, popularly known as the *marshmallow studies*. Originating with a series of experiments conducted by psychologist Walter Mischel at Stanford University between 1968 and 1974, the studies looked at 653 four-year-olds who were individually offered a choice intended to test their ability to delay gratification. Two marshmallows were placed in front of each child, who was then told that he or she was welcome to eat one of the marshmallows now, but if he or she was able to wait until the researcher came back into the room, the child could eat both. Eighty percent of the children could not wait until the researcher returned to the room and went ahead and ate the single marshmallow, but the 20 percent of children able to delay gratification earned the chance to eat both marshmallows.[6]

Years later, these same children were tested on a variety of measures, including capacity for dealing with the emotional trials of adolescence and even their academic performance and SAT scores. The 20 percent of children who more than a decade earlier had opted to wait for the two marshmallows outperformed their adolescent peers on every measure. Follow-up studies conducted when these subjects turned thirty years old continued to show that the delayed-gratification children showed meaningfully better capacities than their peers for pursuing their goals during periods of frustration or stress.[7]

Clearly, the ability to give primacy to one's most profound goals is a crucial factor in leading an effective life, but how does one learn to become better at this? Studies in cognitive psychology provide some clues. Héfer Bembenutty of The City University of New York, Graduate Center, and Stuart A. Karabenick of Eastern Michigan University examined differences in the thought patterns of individuals who were strong at tolerating frustration and those who were not, and discovered a critical causal mechanism behind their behaviors. People who focused their thinking on the object of immediate, or "hot," interest, such as a desire for the immediate pleasure of a sugary snack, were far less likely to hold off on giving in to their impulse.

But the small fraction of people who could delay their gratification actually interpreted the situation in very different terms. Rather than viewing the treat as an opportunity to experience pleasure, they defined the situation as a challenge of willpower. In other words, they reframed the act to be symbolic of their overall willpower and strength of commitment. Those values were much more meaningful to them than the immediate reward of a sugary treat. In this way, they were able to endure the wait.

University of Michigan professors Paul Pintrich and Elizabeth De Groot then conducted a series of studies to examine how to *teach* young students with impulse-control problems how to delay gratification to achieve desirable outcomes. The researchers found that dramatic improvements could occur through the same process of cognitive reconstruction. Teaching children to define delaying gratification as a means to prove their overall willpower and strength led to significantly increased capacities for tolerating uncomfortable sensations in exchange for an eventual, desirable outcome. How individuals interpret the meaning of any exercise and its requisite sacrifices had a powerful influence on their capacity to achieve positive outcomes. Focusing on what tolerating and persevering through difficult affects would prove about their overall strength of character was a very effective means of creating behavior change in individuals with impulsive tendencies.

The same lessons can be seen as applied by the most effective CEOs. Consider how Dave Dillon increased subservience to purpose at Kroger. He told me that of all the subjects we discussed together, subservience to purpose was what probably described his philosophy better than anything else:

> I think [most people] would say [about me] that Dave believes that he's on this earth to be responsible for accomplishing something that is important and bigger than himself, and that that's my mission, that I make subservient everything that's in the way of the mission. I especially make subservient me and my ego and my own desires for whatever it is I might want, because I believe that each of us as human beings want to matter. In order to matter, we need to feel we are attached to something bigger than ourselves. So my attachment that's bigger than me is the mission we're on here at Kroger.

Dillon believes that Kroger's value system that emphasizes the company mission connects to the company's high retention rates among key executive staff: "People feel that we're on a good mission and that they're accomplishing something and are part of something meaningful. I think it's because they feel they're successful here, they feel valued here, they feel part of our mission here. Almost everybody I know has some general belief about why we're here on earth, and I believe that a job is a part of what lets people fulfill why they're here."

It helps Dillon to remember that about 10 percent of the U.S. population goes through Kroger stores every week:

> While I don't think you can take somebody who's had an awful day and turn it into a miracle day, I do think that a smile, a nice

word at the checkout counter, somebody in the supermarket who helps your day go a little easier—I think small gestures like that can go a long way to making our lives and our society and our world a more pleasant place to be. What better mission can there be for an individual than that—having a happier world around them? Almost everybody starts here just for a job. But for the people who stay, it's typically because they like being part of a team, and they like being part of a mission where they feel they've accomplished something, which in this case is serving customers.

Subservience to purpose is a highly learnable attribute. Dillon redefines a person's daily work responsibilities specifically in terms of the crucial role the person plays in pushing forward a larger mission, such as improving the everyday lives of American families. He thereby helps his workers reframe petty frustrations or fatigue into a broader, more meaningful motivation to preserve.

When you are faced with an impulse and are attempting to put it in the right frame, try the exercise suggested in "What Would My Role Model Do?"

What Would My Role Model Do?

Consider the person whom you most admire in your life. Now consider the person you least admire. Whom would you most like to emulate? Next time you are tempted to surrender to a weak impulse—whether it be avoiding conflict or reacting with great emotion to a negative event—before you make your choice, consider how these two individuals would react.

Most readers will find that they are significantly deficient in their level of subservience to purpose. By using a simple exercise such as this one to better manage your distractive impulses through cognitive reconstruction, you can improve the two core aspects of subservience to purpose.

A third essential catalyst to the ability to realize potential is particularly crucial in the dramatically increased complexity of the twenty-first century. It is the ability to find order in chaos, and it is the topic of the next chapter.

6

Finding Order in Chaos
Maintaining Clarity of Thought

Today's leaders must thrive in an environment of unprecedented fluidity, and the ability to find order in chaos is the last of the three catalysts we can employ for combating the turmoil around us. Leaders who can find order in chaos find taking on multidimensional problems invigorating and are distinguished by their ability to bring clarity to quandaries that baffle others. As with the other two central catalysts we have discussed, finding order in chaos has two primary elements: clarity of thought and the drive to solve the puzzle.

Maintaining clarity of thought denotes the way that leaders are able to keep sharp cognitive skills even when the leaders are under pressure. This ability requires affect tolerance regarding fear in particular. Great leaders must be able to think more clearly even as the world becomes more confusing and threatening; they must dampen their anxious emotions and instead focus on intelligent thinking.

Being driven to solve the puzzle means that an individual is compelled by a need to take on challenges that are intimidating to others in scope. Like clarity of thought, this drive has to do with making

Evaluating Your Ability to Find Order in Chaos

As in the previous chapters, the first part of the following exercise should be timed to take no more than two minutes.

Imagine that you work for a large medical-products supply company, and the three-year lease contract for the fleet of cars driven by your salespeople is coming due. You're considering replacing the fleet with hybrid vehicles. Hybrids are appealing, but their lease price is 20 percent higher than standard gasoline cars.

One of your direct reports makes the following comments. How do you respond?

1. In some car accidents, hybrid batteries have been known to rupture and cause injuries.

   a. No form of transportation is perfectly safe.

   b. If the overall rate of injury is substantively higher for hybrids, that would be very relevant.

2. I have a friend who owns a hybrid, and he's had a lot of problems with the electric motor.

   a. We should compare the cost to repair hybrids to the cost of repairing nonhybrids.

   b. Is the hybrid model we are considering less reliable than the conventional model we would otherwise choose?

3. Research published by Greenpeace found that consumers were 30 percent more likely to buy products from companies that were environmentally friendly.

a. The source of this data is so clearly biased that it is rendered irrelevant.

b. If through using hybrids our salespeople would be more likely to make a favorable impression with our customers, then that is a relevant consideration.

4. Recent tests have shown that government fuel economy ratings of automobiles do not reflect the actual fuel economy achieved on the road.

a. This is an excellent example of how hype around a new technology clouds our judgment.

b. The accuracy of the government fuel economy ratings is irrelevant to our decision, particularly since actual fuel economy data is obviously available.

Now turn the timer off, and review all the questions to which you answered "a." Think carefully and deliberately about each of them. Picture yourself as a teaching assistant grading a quiz, and write a brief paragraph explaining to your class why "a" is clearly the better answer. Then do the same thing, this time taking the side of "b." Work on these paragraphs until you feel you have made a definitive case for one answer's being better than the other. For how many questions did you switch your answer to "b"?

For the timed part of the exercise, the more times you answered "b," the higher your ability to maintain clarity of thought. For part two, the higher the proportion of "a" answers you switched to "b" (e.g., two out of three "a" answers switched to "b"), the higher your drive to solve the puzzle.

sense of a seemingly impenetrable mess of data, but it speaks more to a leader's interest and zeal in learning and listening to solve a problem.

Over the next two chapters, we will examine each of these two components of finding order in chaos. But first, try the exercise in "Evaluating Your Ability to Find Order in Chaos" to see where you stand on this catalyst for helping people realize potential.

This chapter will explore how the best leaders keep their thinking clear even in highly stressful and disorganized situations. We'll examine what clarity of thought looks like in practice—and what it doesn't look like. Let's begin by examining how stress affects some people's "intelligence," and how great leaders actually use stress as a motivator for intensifying their focus.

Maintaining Clarity of Thought

The greatest leaders develop a high mental tolerance for the pressures associated with fast-changing, highly complex environments—we call this ability *complex thinking*. They not only know how to keep their wits about them in such situations, but also know how to raise their level of lucidity as the pressure of the situation increases. They become more precise, for example, about setting priorities, understanding component parts, and analyzing data as the circumstances become more critical. As a result, these individuals are willing to place themselves in highly complex, dynamic, and stressful situations time and again because they are gratified by generating clarity where there is confusion. This positive feedback compels them to pursue ever-more audacious undertakings.

Complex thinking is one of the most poorly understood aspects of executive behavior. Although many people believe that intelligence is a fixed attribute, a person making a decision manifests intelligence in myriad ways. In fact, an individual's facility for solving any type of problem is dramatically influenced by the level of agitation the person experiences as he or she makes a decision. In other words, thinking about a problem under pressure is far more complex than if the same problem is presented in a calmer light. In today's competitive environment, aspiring leaders must learn how to confront heightened levels of urgency without allowing that urgency to be disruptive. They must understand how to handle instability, uncertainty, and missteps without collapsing.

Why is this so difficult? The human brain is hardwired to respond to stress physically: the hormonal changes that occur when we experience duress automatically translate stress into heightened muscular function. This same dynamic simultaneously shuts down our complex processing because complex thought slices valuable seconds off the physical response. A valuable automatic trade-off during the days of our fight-or-flight ancestors, this diminution of complex thought during times of stress must be tamed for a leader to be successful in the modern, cerebral business world.

Heightened levels of anxiety have long been shown to dramatically impair people's ability to think, including even the most basic functions such as processing simple information or short-term memory. Regarding more complex tasks, anxiety can most aggressively interfere with people's ability to prioritize tasks, that is, to differentiate between important and irrelevant ones.[1]

In particular, "duress makes people overly focused on the short term—the tyranny of quarterly results that the market presses you on incessantly," explained Ron Daniel, the former managing partner of McKinsey. "That's a huge change over the last twenty years."[2] Daniel said the trick in today's world is learning how to respond to that demand without losing sight of what's required to ensure the long-term vitality of your company. You have to manage under adversity while not becoming totally preoccupied by today's crisis. "You've got to be thinking about how it's going to be when you come out of it, not just six months from now, but six years from now." Yet very few leaders are able to harness this ability to think in a complex fashion under duress.

The Truth Behind Intelligence Tests

In my studies of intelligence testing, I have been repeatedly surprised by just how badly many senior executives do in such testing. During my interviews, I present candidates with a series of real-life case study problems and take them through questions in which they are asked to guide their subordinates and board members to a positive outcome. This requires that the candidates consider the soundness of available data and evaluate the suggestions of their colleagues, while also reconsidering the quality of their own answers to these questions. A full 20 percent of these executives—senior leaders of some of the world's leading businesses—become almost incoherent during this process, unable to provide answers to more than one-third of the questions posed.

But although this inability to think clearly under duress does indeed make them incapable of executing the responsibilities of a chief executive in today's economy, it hardly means that they are stupid. Rather, their response is a reflection of *inadequate training* that renders them cognitively frozen when confronted with both complexity and pressure. This is good news: it means that mastering this attribute is less about becoming smarter or more intelligent—and more about learning how to manifest those traits even when under pressure.

As we learned earlier, we are all made up of a committee of selves. Our identities are an interaction between inherited predispositions and lived experience that are fluid and responsive to the context around us. While it would be much simpler to categorize people as good or bad, smart or stupid, the reality is that *any smart person can be rendered stupid under the right circumstances*. If a person is placed in a context for which he or she is entirely unprepared, and enough pressure is applied that the mind approaches a state of severe agitation, the person's ability to think will simply shut down.

How can leaders bring out their *best* selves in this kind of setting? To lead in today's environment, you must go beyond tolerating stress and fear to actually using them as a *motivator* and tool to enhance your focus and your people's focus.

How Great Leaders Use Stress to Intensify Unity and Focus

Even though it can render intelligent people incapable of complex thought, adrenaline is one of the most useful tools in the human arsenal, and in an environment of ongoing pressure, great leaders must learn how to make this stress hormone an asset. If properly channeled, its presence helps human beings attain levels of performance that they never otherwise would have imagined possible, and after the episode look back in awe at what they were able to do. With the adrenaline gone from their system, people may wonder how their achievement had ever been possible.

Aspiring leaders need to make adrenaline their friend. Making yourself familiar with its presence is key. For example, Larry Hunter and Sherry Thatcher conducted a study of a commission-based financial services sales force.[3] Observing the relationship between the anxiety levels and sales performance of several hundred sales professionals, they found that the revenue numbers of new employees, even strong ones, dropped drastically (average total commissions fell

30 percent) during times of intense pressure. But the performance of the more senior employees, those who had been in the job a few years, noticeably increased (average total commissions rose 50 percent) when they felt the most stress.

In the untrained mind, adrenaline acts as a noisemaker and distracter, causing us to diffuse our attention and increasing the difficulty of focusing on the job at hand. But when we become familiar with the effects of adrenaline, we find ourselves performing with intensified focus. As Marijn Dekkers, CEO of Thermo Fisher, said, "The pressure of an audience is inspiring. It makes you play harder."[4]

Let's look at an example of this kind of practice in real life. Joe Swedish, CEO of Trinity Health Systems, is drawn to helping turn around organizations in crisis. When he became CEO at a regional health system, he faced an urgent situation. Upon his arrival, the hospital was sanctioned by the inspector general of the United States, and soon after, Medicare slapped the hospital with its twenty-three-day notice about the hospital's inadequate care of obstetrics patients. The hospital had twenty-three days to prove that it was correcting the problems, or Medicare would execute the suspension.

"When you are under a twenty-three-day suspension notice, you're staring at the near-death of your organization," Swedish said. "Can you imagine if [the hospital's certification by] Medicare is shut down? You have no business, because commercial [insurers] like Blue Cross and others condition your participation on their contracts to the Medicare certification. It's like ripping the oxygen right out of the scuba diver. You're done."[5]

Swedish's reaction to this pressure? "What a great opportunity," he told me. How many of us could say that, honestly? For most of us, such a crisis would be fodder for the deepest complaints, the most garish of headaches. For Swedish, as a great leader, the burning platform he'd landed on meant a chance to improve everything about how the hospital worked, while providing his people a chance to come together as a group. This change in mind-set is critical to great leaders today.

So how do we get there? Swedish attributes his calm and focused attitude under pressure to his mentors—it wasn't something he was born with; it was something that he learned. "I was the beneficiary of some mentorship experiences that allowed me to feel secure about my ability to respond to forbidding challenges and react to emergencies in an emotional and [procedural] way that is constructive," he said. "That kind of confidence allows you to admit your own vulnerability in these situations. To admit that you don't have all the answers, that you need help. That enables you to learn and be open to advice and counsel, and this is how you use emergencies to build extremely cohesive teams at an accelerated rate."

Thus Swedish used some lessons we've learned while exploring the other attributes—namely, humility and an awareness of the actual circumstances around him, admitting vulnerability as a way to grow. He was able to stay calm in the face of pressure, specifically because he had already practiced admitting vulnerability in the past. This kind of practice makes it possible for leaders to perform under pressure.

Leading Through Pressure

Maintaining calm and focus under pressure is important not just because it allows leaders to make better decisions. Leaders who react under pressure by simply barking out orders miss the critical leadership opportunity that crises bring, Swedish said. "If responded to with confidence and focus, crises can facilitate a mutual dedication amongst your team to solve your problem." Swedish says he's learned to view crises as opportunities for tremendous progress, particularly in building the kinds of dedicated teams that would then play a critical part in turning the hospital into a first-class enterprise. By modeling the correct response to crisis and feeding on the energy that it brings, you can create a context for your people to do the same.

Swedish was fortunate to have mentors who taught him how to tolerate anxiety, and as a result, he developed a means for using adversity to create resilient and powerful teams. His willingness to expose his vulnerability as a leader and to express his need for the help of his colleagues created an authentic unity among his people and him and thus accelerated his colleagues' willingness to support one another's problem-solving efforts. This highly functional collective response helped the group to manage each other's fears more effectively and to use the sense of urgency to better focus on the job at hand.

Another leader who has inspired calm in the eye of the storm of a volatile industry is Dave O'Reilly, the chairman and CEO of Chevron, whom we met earlier in the book. He told me how he keeps his thinking sharp while managing the uncertainty associated with leading an oil company.[6] In his business, which he calls "not for the faint of heart," O'Reilly routinely juggles multibillion-dollar capital investments in risky projects while working in countries that sometimes experience political upheaval.

But O'Reilly told me he doesn't think of these things as pressure. "It's a part of what it means to work in this industry, and maybe it's in the DNA of the company and the people who are in the company," he said. Chevron discovered oil in Saudi Arabia in the 1930s, and more recently, in the early 1990s, it was the first to enter the former Soviet Union to develop oil fields, such as the one Chevron has now in Kazakhstan. "This is a company that was built to manage risk, and I think one of the reasons we're successful is our ability to view the risks we take as informed ones," O'Reilly said.

That history of success and the calm mind-set that O'Reilly chooses have allowed him to stay clearheaded. "If I felt constant pressure about the risk, I wouldn't be able to do this job. In our business, you would immobilize an organization pretty quickly if you didn't have tolerance for risk."

Yet it's one thing to run a risky business like Chevron in a stable economy. What about what the industry faces in the economic upheavals of today? O'Reilly talked about how he counters the agitated mind-set that the current environment seems to magnify. "I quickly and repeatedly point out that nothing that we are seeing today is unprecedented," he told me. "In fact, in almost every example that comes up, I can point to times when it was worse. The things that I see that are actually unprecedented are the positive developments— the advancements of technology and the opportunities they present. That doesn't mean we don't make mistakes or have problems. But it's the big picture regarding how we are doing around the world that matters. You're never batting a thousand, but it's the overall batting average of success that counts."

What Maintaining Clarity of Thought
Looks Like

Dick Keyser, chairman and CEO of W.W. Grainger, Inc., is a walking illustration of what it means to maintain clarity of thought. In 1995, when he first became CEO of Grainger—a global organization that distributes equipment to manufacturers worldwide—conventional wisdom was that business-to-business parts distributors like Grainger would be rendered obsolete by the Internet. Keyser didn't see it that way.

"Things were changing, no doubt about that. The competitive landscape was getting a lot tougher," he said. "But because Grainger had been successful for a very long time, complacency was a much more serious threat than any emerging technology, including the Internet. That's what makes emergencies incredibly useful tools—they get people focused on what matters. If I didn't have real crises, I'd have to make some up."[7]

Crisis forces leaders to boil things down to the essentials of what really needs to get done in order to succeed—and then to pursue those essentials with renewed intensity. "The rise of the Internet was actually just a valuable tool to better clarify why we exist as a business," he said. The Internet taught Keyser that if his company was going to survive, he and his people had to remind themselves why their customers came to them in the first place. Keyser and others at Grainger had to focus on ways to keep improving how they met that need.

"We've had some operational leadership come in and think that the leverage here is cutting costs, and it generally isn't. Sure, you have to keep your costs in line, but everything we sell you can buy anywhere—screwdrivers, wrenches, light bulbs, motors. So why would you buy them from us and why would you pay us more for them than the manufacturer makes on them?" Keyser said. And that, said Keyser, has been the key to his success—engineering service into everything Grainger does:

> We answer the phone—that's our secret weapon—and we really do; you could test that. We have an integrated voice over IP network across the country that makes sure that on the second or third ring, there's a human on there, twenty-four/seven, who can help you. Today, even the phone company doesn't answer its phone.
>
> Service, answering people's questions, getting them the information they need when they need it. That's why people pay us. Challenges like the Internet just help you focus better on what really matters. It cuts through complacency. Success breeds complacency—crisis helps you strip it away.

What Inability to Maintain Clarity of Thought Looks Like

About six years ago, I was in an office building interviewing "Ollie," the CEO of a consumer products company. I had just presented Ollie with a hypothetical crisis that threatened the survival of his business, and was asking him to evaluate data, along with suggestions from colleagues and his board of directors, and to arrive at a sound conclusion about what to do. Having asked these case study questions hundreds of times, I know fairly quickly how well someone is doing, and I could see that Ollie was struggling badly.

It's actually quite remarkable when this happens. Just a few minutes before, when I had asked Ollie about his history with the company, he had confidently articulated the direction he was taking the business. Now he was struggling to offer even the most basic sense of how to proceed in a hypothetical but very plausible, real-world crisis.

These case study questions benchmark individuals on cognitive skills that include evaluating available data and understanding what is known and what more needs to be known to reach a solution. Participants must navigate complex, interpersonal conflicts along the way as they deal with underlying agendas and the likely emotional reactions of the people involved. The vast majority of executives can find their way, but a small number become lost almost immediately. Ollie was lost.

Because we were conducting the interview in English and Ollie's native tongue was German, I had asked a German colleague to join us in case Ollie needed anything translated. Until the case study portion of the interview, our German translator was just observing. But as Ollie became baffled by the case study, the translator tried to help. I would ask Ollie a question, and the CEO would offer an answer that was virtually incoherent, so my colleague, assuming Ollie was simply misunderstanding my question, jumped in to translate into

German what I'd just asked. The translator wanted to ensure that Ollie was not having a language problem. He wasn't.

I knew that Ollie's answers were going to be no better in German than they were in English. I've come to recognize the shift in eye movements, the slight rise in room temperature, and the slight increase in human body odor. These are all the physical responses of someone experiencing an adrenaline flood that is overloading their higher-order functions. Their bodies are prepared to run, not think.

Panic has no cultural boundaries. It looks the same in German, Spanish, or Chinese. My translator was not familiar with this phenomenon, and having seen Ollie answer the questions about his career so competently, he was shocked that Ollie could not seem to find a way to answer some of the most basic aspects of a hypothetical case.

Complicating matters, as we made our way through the case and as Ollie's inability to think under pressure became steadily apparent, my colleague started to visibly react to Ollie's stammering. For instance, I would ask Ollie to respond to a suggestion from a hypothetical subordinate; Ollie would offer an answer that showed no understanding of the flaw in the subordinate's approach, and my colleague would repeat the question in German and Ollie would nod vigorously and repeat the same incoherent answer. At this point, my translator had become so visibly exasperated with Ollie's inability to offer even minimally competent answers to my questions that he began sighing heavily after some responses, rolling his eyes at others. As soon as we finished the first portion of the case, I suggested a brief recess and asked my colleague to step outside.

As soon as we closed the door behind us, my associate launched into a tirade about Ollie's "stupidity." "I cannot believe this moron was made a CEO," he said. I suggested that while Ollie was indeed having an alarming amount of trouble thinking on his feet, my colleague needed to show more composure and respect for Ollie's competence—that when our conversation resumed, there would be no more expressions of frustration about Ollie's answers.

My colleague's reaction was understandable—anyone witnessing Ollie's answers to my questions would shudder at the thought that this person was responsible for a company with revenues over $1 billion. But Ollie was not nearly as incompetent as he appeared during the case study portion of our evaluation. Rather, he had not yet learned to tame the cognitive overload that occurs for people in response to high levels of duress—day-to-day, on the job, he appeared fine: it was when he was confronted with a high-stress crisis that his physical response overcame his mental processes.

But that meant that Ollie wasn't fine—and the numbers proved it. Ollie's company had been performing poorly, and indeed, his was the worst-performing brand in the parent conglomerate's portfolio. This is why I was hired to evaluate Ollie, and now I could understand the reason behind it. Ollie had been promoted to the CEO role at a time when the competitive environment was changing, and he had not been prepared to handle unfamiliar complexity.

But Ollie's reaction to duress provides a critical lesson: human beings are not naturally wired to engage in complex problem solving when they are under duress. As we've said throughout this chapter, *they must be taught how to manage their stress in such a way that it fuels their focus and increases their clarity.* This entails learning how to manage adrenaline without panic and gaining confidence that the sensations that stress induces will not lead to collapse—that on the contrary, these sensations indicate that a heightened level of focus is possible. This kind of reaction can only be gained through experiences that support a person's sense of competence under duress. Ollie had not been given this training and thus was rendered remarkably ineffectual when placed in charge of a large enterprise in a state of flux.

Most often, as in the example of Joe Swedish earlier in this chapter, a leader's training in clearheaded thinking under duress begins with close mentorship. But other kinds of learning can help as well. At the end of the next chapter, I provide some specific suggestions and an exercise for improving your own ability to maintain calmness and clarity in stressful situations and to ultimately realize your fullest potential.

Finding order in the seeming chaos of global commerce requires not only the ability to maintain clarity of thought under pressure, but also another key component: the thirst and thrill that results from pursuing and solving complex puzzles. Global competition and the variables that determine its winners and losers will only get more complex. As we'll see in the next chapter, developing a drive to solve the ever-evolving puzzles as they present themselves and reorganize in new forms is essential to leadership today.

7

Finding Order in Chaos

The Drive to Solve the Puzzle

It was Sunday afternoon, and I was driving with my wife Susan through the Hancock Park neighborhood of Los Angeles. It's one of our favorite weekend activities—our retriever leans his head out the backseat window as we turn down different streets to look at the houses. Mostly we use this time to catch up and talk about what's going on with our lives. This day, we were talking about Susie's dissertation topic.

For several months, she had been working to discover ways that new forms of media could be used to teach children different skills. She was struggling with how her clients' needs were different from her dissertation committee's expectations and whether any paths existed that could make it all come together. I had no answer for her; I could only listen. And at the end of the discussion, she sighed. "And I'm not even sure if there *is* a solution," she said, "or if all of this is just walking down a dead-end road."

People experience tension when they stand at the edge of what is known and yet to be discovered. They feel the pressure and uncertainty of trying to derive a decision that would have profound consequences but for which they have only shifting, incomplete data. In Susie's case, this struggle was intensified by all the effort that she had already put in and the keen understanding of all the effort she would still need to exert to reach a successful outcome—if such an outcome even existed.

Enterprises struggling under these conditions of uncertainty are the most vulnerable; they require a particular kind of tenacity in order to persevere. In today's economy, *all* companies are always at this stage of the game: there is always a critical puzzle to solve, with the uncertainty ahead matched by the resources already spent. But the greatest leaders take advantage of such situations, because they are *driven to solve the puzzle*: they feel at home at this uncertain stage and then drive forward with a solution.

This is the second component of finding order in chaos. Tightly intertwined with clarity of thought, the drive to solve the puzzle is critical for a leader aspiring to move beyond merely the ability to think intelligently in stressful situations. With this drive to solve the puzzle, leaders can create order from the myriad inputs around them. More than ever, leaders must identify what their organization *can* do better than any other organization and what it *should be doing* better than others, and pursue the latter with relentless focus. Fully realizing their own potential and that of their people requires leaders to identify and pursue these types of emerging opportunities through an intense, ongoing thirst for bringing clarity to complex problems.

The key is to see the shifting puzzle of the rapidly evolving competitive space as *stimulating*. As we've seen in all the examples in this book, great leaders' intellectual curiosity combined with a drive to dominate their competitive space enables them to overcome the inevitable stumbles and dead ends that occur and to experience these frustrations as a tightening of the coiled spring that presses the leaders forward toward triumph.

This chapter describes how leaders must have this drive to solve the puzzle if they are to navigate the mazes of today's economy. The drive includes the motivation to learn and to listen. We'll also see examples of what such a leader looks like and doesn't look like. The chapter concludes with suggestions and an exercise for improving your own drive to find a solution and, ultimately, your ability to find order in chaos.

A Thirst for Continuous Learning

The drive to solve the puzzle manifests itself as an intense intellectual curiosity—a love for complex, multidimensional puzzles, and a pleasure in finding solutions to them. Such conundrums can elicit intense sensations: a feeling of uncertain, shifting ground; frustration; anxiety; a struggle to grasp a fleeting answer to a complex question. But leaders who exhibit a deep trust in their ability to manage analytic processes towards a successful conclusion actually enjoy solving this type of challenge.

Kevin Sharer, the CEO of Amgen, compared managing the pressure and complexity of his job to a real-life version of the children's toy Lite-Brite, a game that requires the player to bring together coherent shapes from a random collection of colored bulbs. "The CEO version of Lite-Brite is the ability to instinctively understand what's the right subject," he told me. "What's the right level of detail to talk about that subject? Am I basically a listener? Am I an actor? Am I a director? Am I Socratic? How do I participate in that particular issue?"[1] Asking these kinds of questions is visibly an enjoyable experience for Sharer.

Although he used a game as his analogy, that doesn't mean that he found his job pleasurable immediately. "It's something you have to learn and grow into," he said. Sharer described the CEO job as necessitating asking these questions along three separate axes. There's an activity axis (x) that includes inside things like budget reviews and strategy as well as outside things like dealing with shareholders and regulators. He thinks of the y-axis of the matrix as the level of detail the CEO must apply to an issue: "What were sales on the product this week in a particular geography?" for example, or "What are we going to do for life cycle management for that product?" And the z-axis is the *style* of the CEO—will the executive be hands-on, or will he or she direct the game board from above?

So there are tens of thousands of choices to be made every day. "And you have to instinctively know how to operate around this game board," Sharer said. "The good CEOs have to operate around this cube instinctively, like a flow sport. You know where the ball is. You know who to pass it to. You just know what the flow of the game is. And you've got to have a broad range of capability. This takes time and experience. No one is born knowing how to do this. And you never really finish learning. It's too complex for that. But that's what makes the job so stimulating." Sharer's love of organizing problems to create the best solution is clear in the enthusiasm with which he tackles this analogy. The greatest CEOs all demonstrate this thirst for continuous learning not only about themselves and their roles, but about the complex, real-life puzzles that define today's business environment.

What the Drive to Solve the Puzzle Looks Like

A. G. Lafley, chairman and CEO of Procter & Gamble, is one of these great leaders who is continuously trying to solve every puzzle as a way to drive success. Recently, he was in Brazil on business. Between meetings, he could be spotted down by the river, watching women doing their laundry. Word soon spread about the "crazy gringo" and his unusual sightseeing habits.

"I was trying to understand why our launch of a new detergent for emerging markets had been such a failure," Lafley explained when someone finally asked him about his activities.[2] Market research had suggested that the product should have been a huge hit: knowing that access to clean water was difficult in the developing world, P&G had created a laundry detergent that didn't require a separate rinse cycle for the clothes, which meant much less water needed to get clothes clean. The soap was a major part of the company's strategy to market products to the emerging middle class in those countries—but it hadn't been doing as well as expected.

Lafley's perpetual drive to solve the puzzle at hand spurred him to take advantage of the opportunity he had while in Brazil to study the market personally; his walks down to the river were not crazy strolls but rather his own hands-on version of the market research the company had done earlier. From his adventures, he learned that because the new soap did not create suds during the wash, people didn't feel that the clothes were actually getting clean. "Once we added suds, the product became a huge hit."

Such hands-on work is something Lafley has always enjoyed most about his job. "I am fascinated by people," he told me. "Human beings are incredibly complex and unpredictable, and I'm fascinated by them as consumers and as colleagues and employees."[3] In fact, he sees this as his mission as CEO: connecting the company's strengths with opportunities that it can seize.

A big part of doing that well is listening, he said, and this is a key concept for all leaders who are fueling their drive to solve puzzles. But although many executives consider themselves great listeners, few seem to do this well. I asked Lafley how he learned to engage in such contemplative, open inquiry as a way to solve the conundrums he has faced.

"A lot of it comes from living and working abroad," he said. "If you are in a different culture and you're operating in their language, you have to be a good listener to survive." That goes double for consumer businesses, he said. "Most of the time when I'm in a consumer's home or in a store, I'm listening ninety percent of the time. I'm not standing there asking a mother a list of questions. I'm trying to get her to *tell* me. It's more anthropology than it is interviewing. It's observing. When I sat at the side of the river and watched women do their laundry, I just asked them to tell me what they were doing as they did it. Sometimes I need an interpreter on these trips. But mostly I'm watching, seeking first to understand."

This drive and ability to listen to and learn from others—be they customers, colleagues, subordinates, or family members—is critical for a leader to succeed. Solutions created in a vacuum (without listening to others) are never as good as those with a full range of input; without the drive to solicit that input, a leader is left with subpar answers to tough problems.

How to Solve the Puzzle: Becoming a Masterful Listener

Jim Owens, chairman and CEO of Caterpillar Inc., learned the importance of listening the hard way, earlier in his career at the company. "We had a joint venture that was dysfunctional," Owens said. "After studying it for six months, I came up with a completely different strategic take on it. I thought we should make it into a business unit. I thought it was a pretty innovative idea—we didn't even have business units at the time."[4]

Owens gathered his data and worked with many colleagues in the company to frame the idea. But he admitted that when he met with the individuals who had originally created the venture, he did a very poor job of listening to their feedback. Owens regarded this as the toughest lesson he had to learn when moving from a staff role to a management position.

"Many of them had a lot of pride in what had already been put in place, and with our idea, we had turned the apple cart completely upside down," Owens said. Upon hearing that Owens hadn't taken their ideas into account, his boss sat him down and said that if Owens hoped to become an officer in the company, he'd have to change the way he handled himself. "Sounding like the smartest guy in the room gets you nowhere," his boss told him. "You may think you know what the answer should resemble. But it is arrogance to think that shouldn't be seriously tested. And *along the way, you create the only answer that is viable—the group answer*." Continually searching for the solution to the puzzle means continually listening to those around you to create the smartest answer—which will always be better than *your* smartest answer.

Soon after, that advice would serve Owens well when he was sent to turn around a large, underperforming subsidiary in San Diego, called Solar. The executive team—though made up of terrific individuals—wasn't working well together. In his first strategy conference with the group, Owens decided to take a step back and merely moderate, letting the executives themselves present their knowledge of the business. "At first they all just kind of sat on their hands and stared at me," Owens recalled. "But by the end of the three days, they realized that I didn't come in with the answer. It was really open to debate. And we did—we had great discussions and forged a consensus and got something that we were happy with as a team. We communicated it with vigor and began to drive some terrific results. If I did anything really good there, it was to pull them together to deliver the results in that business." Owens enacted his mastery of listening in such a way that his colleagues were able to learn from it themselves, so that the whole group could excitedly pursue the answer to the puzzle together. By creating a situation in which others could bring their best selves to the table, Owens helped them realize their potential, strengthening the executive team while solving their concerns at the same time.

What a Lack of Drive to Solve the Puzzle Looks Like

You may be reading this chapter and nodding—you may think that you have this drive to solve problems, ask questions, get to the bottom of a knotty issue. But even those individuals who experience this drive often may not invoke it in the most critical—and most difficult—situations. Such situations truly test great leaders, because it is in difficult situations that the drive to solve the puzzle is most important. Let's look at a leader who had this attribute in spades—until the future of his company was at stake.

One of the more interesting parts of my job is helping entrepreneurial founders choose a qualified successor. Entrepreneurs are characterized by an almost obsessive dedication to the success of their business. This is what makes my work with them so fascinating. They believe that they are willing to do whatever it takes to ensure the long-term survival of their business, but when it comes to readying a successor, they invariably do just the opposite.

Entrepreneurs have an almost evangelical belief in the importance of their venture, which is what enabled them to get their business off the ground in the first place. It was their passion for the business that convinced start-up investors that they had the single-mindedness to make it successful. And make no mistake—creating a new company and growing it into *Fortune* 500 status takes a ferocious level of commitment.

In tracing back a founder's company history, we see that each founder has had moments when just about anyone else would have walked away, where the sacrifices required for a business's survival were simply too much. But successful entrepreneurs possess a dedication to their enterprise; their passion pushes them through the darkest times that confront these early days. Much of that zeal often comes from precisely the drive to solve the puzzle. The business itself may be solving the puzzle of how to better serve the needs of a particular market or how to fix a larger problem in society. And certainly, the day-to-day operations of an entrepreneurial firm call for solving puzzles day in and day out. Many entrepreneurs exhibit the highest level of drive for this kind of work.

But here is where a fascinating twist occurs, and why so few entrepreneurs are capable of growing their company into one that lasts long beyond their tenure. Founders have spent so many of their adult years almost obsessively committed to the success of their company that their identity becomes inextricably linked to it. Entrepreneurs tend to create a company that cannot function without them, because they as founders have formed a personal identity that cannot survive without their company. As a result, the idea that anyone within their organization could ultimately render them irrelevant represents a highly destabilizing threat. And so, unlike most founders' performance in other areas of the company, when it comes to succession, the entrepreneurs' drive to solve the puzzle is nearly always totally absent.

"Terry," the founder, chairman, and CEO of an extraordinarily successful, midsize financial services firm, is an excellent example of this phenomenon. He contacted my company after reading an article about how all the best CEOs always have specific plans in place for their own retirement. This article stressed that great CEOs commit a significant amount of their time to developing someone who could take their place, and they spend several years preparing this person for the job.

Terry was intensely devoted to his company and asked us to help him ensure that he was making adequate preparations for his eventual departure. But upon our review of his leadership team and potential successors, it was clear that there was no one remotely qualified among them to take his place. Talking to his board members, we discovered they could not imagine the company without Terry. As one board member described it, when Terry walked into a room, all eyes went to him. He was so passionate and charismatic, it was as if he "sucked all the air out of the space."

In a sense, this is what founder entrepreneurs actually do, without knowing it. Their intensity, which served them so well in fighting their way through the obstacles of starting a new venture, tends to repel other strong, highly talented leaders from wanting to work alongside them. This is further aggravated by entrepreneurs' tendency to resist relinquishing any significant decision-making authority in the business. As a result, they draw "sidekick" colleagues. The team that Terry formed around him was just that way, highly deferential to his authority. Among his people, not one individual was remotely prepared or qualified to replace him.

The only possible contender, in any other circumstance, might have been "Bryson." Intensely bright and driven, he did an exceptional job running the company's biggest division. Yet he was a social introvert who didn't naturally draw attention. Although Terry told me that he agreed that Bryson was an obvious choice, Terry didn't think the board would ever accept Bryson as CEO. Why? Because Terry had asked Bryson, as his potential successor, to give a presentation to the board. "It went horribly," Terry said. "Bryson completely flopped. He's a nonstarter as a candidate." The board had asked him some tough questions, and Bryson kept freezing up. This went on for forty-five minutes, and it killed his image as a possible contender.

When I pressed Terry further, I discovered that this was Bryson's first time presenting to a board and that Terry hadn't help him prepare for the meeting in any way. "I wanted the board to see and evaluate Bryson as he really is," he explained.

Terry wasn't aware that he had actually used Bryson's presentation to the board to do the opposite of his stated intention. By putting Bryson, a man not naturally suited to public speaking, in front of a highly aggressive board with absolutely no preparation, Terry was virtually guaranteeing that the incident would go badly. Further, when the presentation did begin to unravel, Terry did nothing to step in and prevent any serious damage. He allowed Bryson, the most obvious choice to succeed him, to bury himself in the board's eyes as a potential successor.

Even though these intentions were very much unconscious, Terry effectively used this exercise to prove to everyone his own critical role to the company's survival. It's understandable; to do otherwise would be to prove to everyone that Terry was not vitally needed anymore, a conclusion that would deeply disrupt Terry's sense of identity and purpose. If Terry was to implement a thoughtful and effective succession process, he would first have to confront the complex dynamics that were making him unable to let go. Thus far, he had shown himself motivated to solve every puzzle—except the critical puzzle of his own replacement.

By ignoring a critical puzzle, leaving it to Bryson to figure out on his own how to impress an aggressive board, Terry undermined his true goals of achieving his greatest potential and that of his people as well. Without the true drive to solve a puzzle, that problem will not get solved. Similarly, your own company will never be able to identify what it can do better than anyone else, and figure out how, without your drive behind it.

Given that we are all a committee of selves, Terry's behavior should come as no surprise, however; we all bring forth different selves in different situations. Though Terry loved to solve problems, here was a puzzle that he did not truly *want* to solve. To realize your full potential, you must first recognize these moments when you are not exhibiting an attribute that is usually one of your strengths and ask why.

Improving Your Capacity for Finding Order in Chaos

So how can you face situations with multiple inputs and maintain both intelligent thought and your own drive to solve the problem? The key to both is experience and an *awareness* of that experience. That awareness can increase your confidence to a level that allows you to embrace the drive to solve the puzzle and get the right answer.

Confidence is like railroad tracks in the brain. They get laid down over time, and they allow us to approach something with the sense that we've been there before and we can do it. The positive feedback we get from maintaining clarity under pressure gives us a thirst for more situations that involve such pressure, and we are thus driven to solve the puzzle. At their core, this is how the two attributes—clarity under pressure and the drive to solve the puzzle—are intertwined.

A series of examples from my own experience will show how finding order in chaos can be a learned attribute. My goal here is not to put myself forward as an example of a great leader—but rather to show how all of us can become aware of and develop these attributes through our own experiences of stressful, chaotic situations, learning to be confident throughout those moments.

In 1982, Great Britain had just invaded the Falkland Islands in a bid to wrest them from Argentinian control. The war was controversial, a long-standing dispute over territory. My sixth-grade teacher, Mrs. Sullivan, had set up a debate in which we, the students, would discuss the merits of each side. Three students were on the Argentinean side, and three, including me, were to argue for Great Britain's point of view. We would debate in front of the whole class, and the class would publicly grade us on our performance and declare a winner.

I was new to the class and was not particularly well liked. My confidence was already low when I was told I'd be speaking last. As the other students spoke, they went over all the arguments that had been covered in the news for weeks: Argentina's historical right to the land, charges of British bullying. When it was my turn to speak, I asked the class what I thought was a straightforward question and maybe a new way of thinking about the problem: "American Indians occupied the land that most of our houses are on today. If an American Indian walked up to your front door today and said, 'You and your family have to leave; I have an ancestral right to this land,' would you do it? Would you leave? Does that Indian have a right to your home?"

I thought this was a pretty smart approach and different from everything that I'd heard in the news and that my parents and their friends were saying. But suddenly, I looked over at the teacher. I was shocked. There was a look of incredible distaste on her face, and she deliberately shook her head in disapproval.

I was floored. This was the first time she had not given a supportive nod to the speaker. The rest of the class, including my team members, could see it, too. What would they think of me? Obviously, they weren't happy; one hissed at me, "Justin, how could you say that? Say something else. You're going to make us lose." I was suddenly completely confused, lost. What had I done wrong? How could I have stumbled so badly? I could only mumble a defeated response, "I have nothing else." Lacking the confidence to press through the aggressively disconfirming reaction of an authority figure, I collapsed and went silent.

Just a few weeks later, I was sitting restlessly at a dinner my parents were hosting. They had invited over a number of faculty members—both my parents were professors at Johns Hopkins University—and I always dreaded these dinners, the formal manners they required of me, and the battles for intellectual supremacy that inevitably dominated the conversation.

But this night was different. It would give me a special gift, a memory that I would later use to overcome the kinds of fears that had overwhelmed me in the Falklands debate. My father suddenly turned the attention at the table to me. "Justin, say something smart." Now, I don't remember what I said in response. But I *do* remember really feeling that my father was proud of my mind, and that really meant something.

My father taught pulmonary medicine at the medical school. To say that he was intellectually confident would not do him justice. He was an argumentative contrarian on any issue, speaking his mind with seeming certainty that his perspective was correct. But he would often get a twinkle in his eyes when I would tell him why I thought he was wrong about something. My mind seemed capable of tickling him, and his positive responses to my own intellectual efforts gave me the internal confidence that whatever I might say in the moment would be well received. Later in life, I've realized that to whatever degree I'm intellectually confident under pressure (and to whatever degree I've grown from that intimidated kid in the classroom), it was largely because of my dad's behavior, like that night with the faculty. It's that confidence that allows me to really have fun pursuing a question or an idea, even in what could be the most stressful situations.

For example, much more recently, I was given the opportunity to speak to an advisory board of my company, Spencer Stuart. The board was made up of an intimidating lineup of many of my longtime personal heroes. The meeting dragged on—I was slated to speak at the very end—and I could feel the minutes ticking away. Would they get to me? Would they not? I had every excuse for a great case of nerves.

But when my turn came, I was able to conjure up confidence because of my years of speaking in front of tough audiences— Mrs. Sullivan and my father chief among them. I spoke about what it meant to be a CEO—specifically that being a leader was just as much about being able to elicit sharp answers from others as being able to come up with them oneself. At the end of my presentation, one of the board members stood up and declared to the room, "That's it. You've nailed the job of the CEO." Others around the table nodded.

Despite the surreal feeling of sitting in the room with these people, listening to them discuss the current trends in the business world and how they affected our company, knowing I was about to get the chance of a lifetime to show my stuff to some of the greatest minds in my field—despite all that—I was able to maintain cogent thought, perform at my best, and truly enjoy the experience. When I think back on that moment, the pressure, I remember a surprising *lack* of nerves. In fact, it was just the opposite: I felt like a kid in a candy store, so excited for the opportunity, so curious to discover what new places their minds would take me. In the heat of the moment, I was driven to solve the puzzle, because of all my preparation and because my learned confidence allowed me to engage intellectually under pressure. I was able to engage those I was leading—in this case the board—with my ideas because of my ability to find order in chaos. And improving our own capacity to fight through moments of stupidity and find order in chaos begins with just this kind of awareness of our own ability to improve ourselves.

The exercise presented in the box "States of Pressure" will help you strengthen your ability to perform and be stimulated under pressure. Essentially it depends on memorizing something—which could be a poem, mathematical formulas, historical dates, or anything—and

States of Pressure

Memorize the names of all fifty states until you can consistently recite them in two minutes or less. Then tell a family member or your best friend about your new trick and do it for him or her, in front of a timer. You'll probably find that the added stress of having an audience—even someone you know and feel comfortable with— trips you up. But repeat it a few more times until you are able to perform consistently in under the amount of time allowed.

Now, at your next dinner out with friends, tell them that if you are able to do your trick they will pick up your share of the tip. Have one person keep time, and command the rest to mock you if you stumble along the way. Again, with a larger group ready to taunt any mistakes, you are less likely to have a perfect run. But repeat this exercise at several more dinner parties, and you'll again be able to consistently run through all fifty states in less than two minutes, regardless of distractions you encounter. Eventually, you will find that you can do this exercise faster, with more accuracy, in front of an audience than when you are doing the same by yourself.

Then, the next time that you are in a situation in which you are tense because you need to perform under stressful circumstances, remember how you have shed the habit of making mistakes simply because of added pressure. It takes practice, as we have learned, to calm the nerves and be able to solve complex problems in stressful situations.

being able to recite it under increasingly stressful situations in which your peers judge you. It is a microcosm of the experiences you will undergo as a leader; your success in exercises like this can begin building the confidence and self-awareness you need to release your intellectual capacities in tough situations.

Your ability to find order in chaos, like the other two catalysts that enable you to realize potential, is a skill and a mind-set that you must learn and reinforce over a lifetime. For too long, leaders have abdicated their role in the success or failure of their people, wishfully assuming that their people's success was a consequence of others' inherent inadequacies, not a reflection of interactive exchange between subordinate and leader. In the complex, interactive economy of the twenty-first century, excellence will come from leaders who recognize that the previous, unidirectional assumption of leadership is obsolete and who take advantage of this knowledge. The next and final chapter offers a capstone example of a maestro CEO who employs all three catalysts for realizing potential in a global economy.

8

Setting the Virtuous Flywheel in Motion

Throughout this book, I have challenged the notion that human beings are fixed entities whose behaviors can be understood as existing distinct from their situation. Complexity theory and interactionist models reveal human identity to be a fluid, cocreated interaction between individuals and their environment. The implications for leadership are striking. Because the patterns of people's behaviors are undeniably a reflection of their interaction with the system that has been created around them, their success or dysfunction is very much a consequence of the patterns of that system. No longer can people in positions of authority disregard their profound role in their people's performance, or lack thereof. The three catalysts described in this book are the key to allowing people's best selves to emerge in an environment of ongoing duress, enabling them to realize their potential.

As a final summary, let's look at how a master of the CEO role in the twenty-first century, Dave Dillon of Kroger, elucidates all three catalysts for realizing potential in a global economy. The first of the catalysts, *realistic optimism,* represents a person's ability to recognize risks while still remaining confident that these challenges can be overcome. Dillon described what this factor looks like amid the recurring stress of discounter pricing threats, major labor strikes, and the massive economic downturn of the late 2000s.

"It's almost like you bifurcate your brain," he told me. "In half of my brain, I am scared every day, almost all the time, about what I see out there as threats. The economy right now, if I would let it, could have me absolutely on the edge. The other half of my brain is saying these things are just obstacles to be overcome, things to be fixed. I've never found a problem, really, that I thought was insurmountable. There's lots of bogeymen out there, and I think I see them for what they are: they are genuine and they have the capacity to derail a company even as big as Kroger. But I believe, and I've seen, that anything that is a big problem can be solved."[1]

Dave Dillon shows us a living example of realistic optimism at its finest—that a leader can possess a clear sense of the risks confronting a business without becoming overwhelmed by them. There is nothing more empowering for a team facing a serious threat than having a leader who helps them face the complexities of the threat as they truly exist, but who does so with an unshakable faith that ultimately, by walking through the fire together, the team and the company will prevail.

Next, Dillon reveals his deep *subservience to purpose,* the second of the three catalysts that determine leaders' capacity for realizing potential in themselves and their people. Dillon assembled a leadership team of individuals who possessed a shared dedication—to pursue the noble cause of continuously improving the affordability and ease with which Americans could buy groceries. His success in doing so is reflected in the tremendous commitment he has earned from his team: over the last ten years, among the approximately thirty-five top positions at Kroger, Dillon has lost five people to competitive jobs. Each of them left for nothing less than to become CEO of a new company, he told me.

"Most people may come here for a job, but they stay because of our mission. Ten percent of the people in this country go through one of our stores every week to buy groceries for their families. We are here to find a way to make their lives better," Dillon said.

When an organization has dominated its industry as Kroger has, its senior team is repeatedly offered opportunities to leave. But by clearly defining the meaningful role that Kroger's work played in improving the lives of American families, Dillon generated retention rates that were unusually high. Such loyalty is substantive evidence that Dillon successfully brought and kept together a group of individuals who were unusually committed to the company—a symptom of the strong subservience to purpose that he has facilitated.

Finally, Dillon exhibits the third attribute of leaders who are able to realize potential, *the ability to find order in chaos.* In today's global economy, the number of variables that affect a business has sharply increased. It is up to a leader to find clarity amid this seeming chaos, to cull a potentially overwhelming breadth of data into the conclusions that matter most. Dillon told me how, in the late 1990s, he initiated a strategy of aggressive price cuts, and in response, Wall Street nearly halved Kroger's stock price. But a few years later, the growth of discount stores like Wal-Mart proved these price cuts to be critical and prescient.

Dillon had spotted that bit of clarity in a forest of annual reviews from his vendors. "Those meetings would cover a lot of issues and data," he said. "One of the things that came up was that we had lost a point or two of market share that year on beauty supplies or health products to the discounters. And I vaguely remembered that the year before, we'd been told the same thing." Yet at the time, these little shifts weren't seen as that significant, because Kroger was still growing nicely overall and hitting all its earnings targets.

But for Dillon, these shifts did have significance: "It nagged at me. So I went and found some data that showed market share for the entire supermarket industry. And in toilet tissue, paper towels, health and beauty care, pet food, cleaning supplies, laundry detergent—all of those things had gradually shifted towards discounters." Dillon discovered that in an eight-year period, the industry had lost 20 percentage points of its market share in each of those categories.

"That's a gigantic shift. The amazing thing was, we'd hear these annual reviews and they didn't make any sense to us," he said. "We saw the general directional shift, but we did not realize how significant it had been until we looked at an eight-year trend of our industry as a whole." That's when Dillon saw that sales were going to crash in a couple of years if he didn't do something.

The multitude of competitive threats coming from new, previously unrelated sources has dramatically increased the volume of data a leader must sift through to find the means to ongoing survival. Dillon's capacity for seeing the most relevant facts that will affect his company's future is essential to his facilitating his team's triumph over Kroger's competition.

Dillon offers a prime example of an individual who has mastered the recursive process of realizing potential within the twenty-first century, both in himself and in others. This facility represents the central responsibility of any leader—the core organizing principle that must underlie everything you do. Although we all have an innate drive to realize potential, we are not born knowing exactly how to do it. The attributes, or catalysts, that enable us to realize potential must be encouraged until they are internalized. Once you experience the gratification of triumph in the pursuit of meaningful goals, the virtuous cycle of realizing potential becomes a regenerating flywheel that is transmitted to others.

Yet the key attributes for bringing out the best in yourself and your people must begin somewhere. This book represents a starting point, a way of understanding how to cultivate this innate thirst that human beings possess to better themselves.

It begins with leaders learning how to do so themselves. Because if there is one critical takeaway to be learned from this book, it is that *people do not act as isolated entities, but are reflections of an essential interaction between themselves and the context in which they are placed.* Leaders cannot simply give instructions to their people about how to master their potential in a world of duress. A person's potential can only emerge as an active process, consciously cultivated through a fluid, on-going exchange between leaders and their people. And the exchange utilizes the three essential catalysts that make it possible. This book offers insights into both the key organizing principles that govern the psychology of leaders who have mastered this process and how they did so.

Finally, the management sciences must move beyond their overly simplistic, reductionist views of human beings and join other disciplines in their exploration of how complexity theory can enrich and deepen understandings of truth. Through these interactionist models, we can far more accurately understand the causes of professional success and, consequently, achieve that very success ourselves.

Notes

Introduction

1. Joseph Bower, *The CEO Within: Why Inside Outsiders Are the Key to Succession Planning* (Boston, MA: Harvard Business School Press, 2007).

2. Larry Bossidy, telephone interview with author, October 2009.

3. David Dillon, telephone interview with author, April 2009.

4. David Novak, telephone interview with author, June 2009.

5. Herb Kelleher, telephone interview with author, June 2009.

6. Andrea Jung, telephone interview with author, May 2008.

7. Throughout the book, I use pseudonyms for some of the CEOs I discuss in the book, to ensure their anonymity. The first time these CEOs are mentioned in a chapter, I place quotes around the pseudonym.

8. Kelleher, telephone interview with author, 2009.

Chapter 1

1. Fred Hassan, interview with author, Kenilworth, NJ, July 2009.

2. Mihaly Csikszentmilhalyi, *Creativity: Flow and the Psychology of Discovery and Invention* (New York: Harper Collins, 1996).

3. Ralph Larsen, interview with author, New York, NY, March 2008.

4. A. G. Lafley, interview with author, Cincinnati, OH, May 2009.

5. Herb Kelleher, telephone interview with author, June 2009.

6. Jim Skinner, telephone interview with author, June 2009.

7. Marijn Dekkers, interview with author, Boston, MA, June 2009.

Chapter 2

1. Bond rating agency statement release, 2007.

2. Miles White, telephone interview with author, April 2009.

3. Kevin Sharer, interview with author, Thousand Oaks, CA, August 2009.

Chapter 3

1. David O'Reilly, interview with author, San Ramon, CA, June 2009.

2. Robert White, "Motivation Reconsidered: The Concept of Competence," *Psychological Review* (September 1959): 297–333.

3. Edward L. Deci and Richard M. Ryan, "The General Causality Orientations Scale: Self-Determination in Personality," *Journal of Research in Personality* 19, no. 2 (June 1985): 109–134.

4. The power of goal setting and prompt, reliable feedback systems has been proven in hundreds of studies. Edwin A. Lock, Karyll N. Shaw, Lise M. Saari, and Gary P. Latham, "Goal Setting and Task Performance: 1969–1980," *Psychological Bulletin* 90, no. 1 (July 1981): 125–152, reviewed twelve years of goal setting and feedback studies and concluded that 90 percent of all findings show that goal setting and performance feedback quantifiably increased motivation and performance.

5. Chris Van Gorder, interview with author, San Diego, CA, January 2009.

Chapter 4

1. Miles White, telephone interview with author, March 2009.

2. Larry Bossidy, telephone interview with author, October 2009.

3. Ralph Larsen, interview with author, New York, NY, April 2009.

Chapter 5

1. Jim McNulty, interview with author, Pasadena, CA, spring 2007.

2. Raymond Milchovich, interview with author, Livingston, NJ, July 2009.

3. "Barack Obama: How He Did It," *Newsweek,* November 5, 2008.

4. Chris Van Gorder, interview with author, San Diego, CA, January 2009.

5. Fred Smith, telephone interview with author, May 2009.

6. Walter Mischel, Yuichi Shoda, and Monica Rodriguez, "Delay of gratification in children," *Science,* (May 1989): 933-938.

7. Ozlem Ayduk, "Delay of gratification in Children," Contributions to social-personality psychology, in *Persons in Context: Building a Science of the Individual,* eds. Yuich Shoda, Daniel Cervone, and Geraldine Downey (New York: Guilford Press, 2007), 97–109.

Chapter 6

1. Nazanin Derakshan and Michael W. Eysenck, "Anxiety, Processing Efficiency, and Cognitive Performance: New Developments from Attentional Control Theory," *European Psychologist* 14, no. 2 (2009): 168–176.

2. Ron Daniel, interview with author, New York, NY, March 2009.

3. Larry W. Hunter and Sherry M. B. Thatcher, "Feeling the Heat: Effects of Stress, Commitment, and Job Experience on Job Performance," *Academy of Management Journal,* 50, no. 4 (August 2007): 953–968.

4. Marijn Dekkers, interview with author, Boston, MA, September 2007.

5. Joe Swedish, telephone interview with author, October 2008.

6. Dave O'Reilly, interview with author, San Ramon, CA, May 2009.

7. Dick Keyser, telephone interview with author, April 2009.

Chapter 7

1. Kevin Sharer, interview with author, Woodland Hills, CA, August 2009.

2. A. G. Lafley, interview with author, Cincinnati, OH, May 2009.

3. A. G. Lafley, interview with author, Cincinnati, OH, May 2009.

4. Jim Owens, interview with author, Peoria, IL 2009.

Chapter 8

1. Dave Dillon, telephone interview with author, April 2009.

Index

About the Author

Justin Menkes is an acclaimed author and leading expert in executive assessment. A consultant for the elite executive search firm Spencer Stuart, he advises the boards of the world's leading companies on their choice of CEO. His clients include Chevron, Blackstone, Mass Mutual, and State Street. He authored the *Wall Street Journal* bestseller *Executive Intelligence: What All Great Leaders Have* and has written articles for *Chief Executive* and *Harvard Business Review*. During his doctoral work at Claremont Graduate University, Justin studied under the late Peter Drucker. He graduated with honors from Haverford College and received his MA in psychology from the University of Pennsylvania. Menkes holds a PhD in organizational behavior from Claremont Graduate University.

This industry is great because it allows you to make a difference. Always do one or two things more than you are asked. Choose to enjoy what you do - figure out how to make it so.

IPC

1) skill, knowledge
2) put pieces together
3) long term strategic thinking
4) Temperment - no drama, no cynics, not selfish
5) Value - where do you want to be, what are your goals - not everyone wants to be CEO - that's good!

Strengths

listening, communicate strategy with passion, invest in picking good people

Challenges

seeing the solution and not having patience to bring others along, not willing to "grow" or "nurture" those who say they cant figure it out or bring their A game, communicating the vision to help bring them along

You dont win on strategy, you win on execution - but execution of a strategy